Responsive Classroom

Interactive Modeling

A Powerful Technique for Teaching Children

Margaret Berry Wilson

NORTHEAST FOUNDATION FOR CHILDREN, INC.

The stories, lesson plans, and scripts in this book are all based on real events in the class-room. However, to respect the privacy of students, names and identifying characteristics have been changed.

All net proceeds from the sale of this book support the work of Northeast Foundation for Children, Inc. (NEFC). NEFC, a not-for-profit educational organization, is the developer of the *Responsive Classroom*® approach to teaching.

ISBN: 978-1-892989-53-6
Library of Congress Control Number: 2012939544

Cover and interior photographs © Jeff Woodward. All rights reserved.

Cover and book design by Helen Merena

Northeast Foundation for Children, Inc.
85 Avenue A, P.O. Box 718
Turners Falls, MA 01376-0718

800-360-6332
www.responsiveclassroom.org

Third printing 2014

Printed on recycled paper

Contents

✳

Introduction

✳

Have you ever tried to learn something by having someone tell you or quickly show you how to do it, only to discover that you can't remember what they said or did? That's exactly what happened to me when I tried to learn how to make my mother's amazing fudge.

I had the recipe—my mother allegedly wrote down what to do. But, in my kitchen, 2,000 miles from hers, it just wasn't working the way the recipe said it should. So I called her and she explained what to do. But, sure enough, as soon as I got off the phone, her verbal advice did not make as much sense as it had when I'd been listening. And it didn't help my fudge.

Then, when I visited with my mom a few months later, I asked her to show me how to make her fudge. Perhaps because she had made it hundreds of times before, she whipped together the ingredients and spouted off directions so quickly that my head was spinning. Back home, I tried again, but I still could not get my fudge to come out the way hers did. To this day, my mother's fudge remains elusive to me.

So what would it really take for me to learn how to make that great fudge? I wish my mother and I could make it side by side. Yes, she would have to slow down to teach me—and be there to coach me when I tried to copy her. But I think that through a combination of her demonstrating and my trying things out while she coached me, I could do it. (If only I could get my mother to agree to this. Secretly, I think she doesn't want me to be able to make her fudge so that hers will always be best. But that's another story!)

After all my failures with the fudge, I couldn't help but think of how similar my experience was to students' experiences in many classrooms, especially when it comes to learning new routines and skills. No matter how often we teachers repeat directions, students seem to miss some steps. That's because they tend to tune out more and pay attention less when we just repeat the same directions over and over again.

Perhaps more problematically, repeating how to do things again and again feels very negative to teachers and students. Teachers' frustration reveals itself in our tone, demeanor, and words as we nag, cajole, or plead with students to remember how to do even basic tasks. Naturally, students *feel* nagged, cajoled, or annoyed. That was how my students and I felt before I learned about Interactive Modeling, an essential practice of the *Responsive Classroom*® approach to teaching.

A Step-by-Step Approach

Interactive Modeling is a straightforward, seven-step technique that's very effective for teaching procedures and routines, such as walking safely in the hallway, and social and academic skills, such as listening respectfully and highlighting important ideas in a text. Parents and coaches can also use this technique to teach children skills, from putting dishes away carefully to running the bases safely. In brief, Interactive Modeling is a great way to teach any routine or skill that needs to be done in one specific way (for safety, efficiency, or other reasons).

Instead of assuming that if we tell children how to do something enough times they'll "get it," Interactive Modeling *shows* students exactly how to do what we expect. It has built-in steps that help students notice for themselves the details of how a behavior looks and sounds. And it has built-in steps for practicing and for receiving teacher feedback during this practice. This powerful combination of noticing and practice enables students to engage more deeply with their learning and remember more.

On the next page, you can read about a seven-step Interactive Modeling session I did with second graders after I learned this technique. My goal was to teach the children how to sit and show they were listening at circle time—something they had been struggling with since the start of school.

1 Say what you will model and why.

I tell the class: "To learn and show how much we care for each other, we all need to listen when someone else is talking. I'm going to show you what listening looks like on the rug. Watch what I do."

2 Model the behavior.

Without talking, I sit down at a spot on the rug, legs crossed, hands in lap, and back straight. I face my empty teacher chair and lean slightly toward it. Then I nod a little.

3 Ask students what they noticed.

"What did you notice me doing?" I ask. "You were nodding your head" and "Your mouth was closed," they say. "What else was I doing?" I prompt, until all the key elements of my demonstration are named.

4 Invite one or more students to model.

"Who can show us how to listen the way I showed you?" I ask. Angela volunteers. She carefully folds her legs and puts her hands in her lap. And just as I did, she leans forward and nods.

5 Again, ask students what they noticed.

"How did Angela sit and listen?" The children report that she was looking at the teacher chair, sitting with her legs crossed, and nodding. One student says, "She did it just like you!"

6 Have all students practice.

"Now, let's see if we all can show how to sit and listen the way you just saw it done," I say. The students all demonstrate careful sitting and listening.

7 Provide feedback.

"That's it! You all did exactly what you saw demonstrated. You sat up straight with legs crossed. Hands were in laps and eyes on the teacher chair. Lots of you were nodding. It looks like we are ready to learn. Let's read a mystery book and see how we do at listening."

Soon after, I noticed the difference Interactive Modeling made to the children's behavior and to our classroom climate at circle time. But I also saw how this improvement carried over to all the other times that children needed to listen—and that's when I grasped the power of this technique. Since then, many teachers have told me that once they tried Interactive Modeling, they couldn't imagine teaching without it.

For instance, my friend and colleague Lara told me about her experience with cafeteria trays. Year after year, she had instructed students to clear 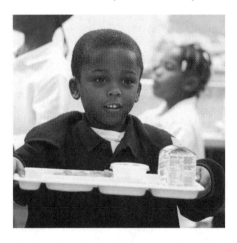 their trays off into the trash can and then stack them up neatly. On most days, however, what Lara saw as her class rushed out of the cafeteria were trays with trash still on them, stacked in a heap. Sometimes, Lara would inwardly groan at the extra work she and her students were leaving for the cafeteria staff. Other times, she would "fuss" at students about doing it again or doing it better. Either way, the end of lunch was often soured and the transition back to classroom learning strained.

Then, Lara decided to use Interactive Modeling. And, at last, her students "got it." On most days, all the trays were now cleared off and neatly stacked. The cafeteria staff noticed, too. As is typical in many schools, they assumed that Lara had a "really good class" that year. But "good" classes don't happen by chance! After years of struggling with this routine, Lara knew that it was her new teaching practice—Interactive Modeling—that had made all the difference.

More Time for Learning

Interactive Modeling's seven-step format makes these lessons fast-paced and easy to teach. The shortest might take just a few minutes, and a complex Interactive Modeling lesson might take twenty minutes or so. If you were modeling for younger students how to put the top on a marker, you could teach the entire modeling lesson within three to four minutes. If you were teaching older students how to partner chat about a shared reading, including time for students to discuss a selection, the entire lesson might take fifteen or twenty minutes.

From experience, I know that even a small investment of time in doing Interactive Modeling is worth it. You'll actually *gain* time by doing Interactive Modeling. Students will spend more time on task, focused on their learning. You'll have more time for academics and teaching because students will ask fewer procedural questions. Think about how many times you're interrupted each day, how many times you have to repeat directions—and how draining that can be. Yes, it does take a leap of faith to start using Interactive Modeling as one of your main teaching practices. But when you do, you'll see a big difference in the life of your classroom and in the amount of teaching and learning that takes place.

For All Teachers

Interactive Modeling works for younger and older students. So, any classroom teacher can use Interactive Modeling, as can teachers of special education, teachers of English language learners, and special area teachers, including art, music, foreign languages, PE, technology, and library. Administrators and other school leaders can also use the practice to teach expected behaviors in whole-school settings, such as what to do at an assembly.

For Teaching Many Skills

You can use Interactive Modeling to teach a wide range of routines and skills that students need to use repeatedly throughout the school year. This technique is especially useful at the beginning of the year, when you're establishing expectations and helping students learn new skills, but you can rely on it all year long. Parents and coaches can also use this technique to reinforce skills children learn at school and to teach new ones. Once you start to use this technique, you can use it to teach whichever routines and skills are essential for your students.

INTERACTIVE MODELING CAN HELP YOU TEACH:

Procedures and Routines

- Cleaning up and putting away math manipulatives
- Lunch skills and routines
- Moving chairs and desks
- Recess skills and routines
- Responding to signals for quiet attention
- Schoolwide assembly routines
- Shelving classroom library books
- Snack procedures
- Start-of-day and end-of-day routines
- Storing backpacks and other items in cubbies or lockers
- Storing playground equipment
- Using art supplies, such as glue sticks and scissors
- Transitioning from one area of the classroom to another
- Transitioning from one classroom to another
- Using the bathroom
- Using the pencil sharpener
- Walking in the hallway

Social and Academic Skills

- Asking and responding to questions
- Completing work and getting ready for the next lesson
- Following a math algorithm
- Greeting people
- Heading one's paper (name, date)
- Listening
- Making and responding to comments
- Proofreading a piece of writing
- Reading and following test directions
- Recording results or observations in a science class or on a form
- Signaling readiness to participate in a classroom activity
- Sounding out words
- Taking part in a whole-group discussion
- Turning and talking with a partner
- Using and organizing notebooks
- Using technology resources
- Working in a small group
- Working with a partner
- Working with a cross-grade reading buddy

Why Interactive Modeling Works

Interactive Modeling works because it combines critical elements of effective teaching—modeling positive behaviors, engaging students in active learning, and assessing their understanding throughout the lesson. These elements help students achieve greater, faster, and longer-lasting success in meeting expectations and mastering skills. Here's more on why Interactive Modeling works:

Students learn why the routine or skill is important. The teacher briefly states why doing a routine or procedure as taught connects to the classroom rules and is essential to their learning. She then reinforces the reasons throughout the Interactive Modeling lesson. Knowing why a routine or skill matters increases students' motivation to become experts at it.

Students create a clear mental image of what's expected. Interactive Modeling intentionally builds in opportunities for children to see several accurate models of the desired behavior. These multiple opportunities enable students to develop one clear picture of what to do. In traditional modeling approaches, teachers often show students what to do just once, leaving many students with incomplete mental images. Worse, if the teacher uses negative modeling (showing students what *not* to do), students form a competing mental picture that is often more powerful than the positive image the teacher intended to create. In Interactive Modeling, only the positive (what *to* do) is modeled.

Students do the noticing. In Interactive Modeling, it's not the teacher who points out what students need to know; it's the students themselves. They're responsible for noticing the details as they observe the demonstrations given by the teacher and student volunteer(s). Throughout the modeling, students have multiple opportunities to watch, listen, and analyze. They get the message that they are important, that their observations matter. This sense of importance, combined with opportunities to talk, listen, and practice, naturally leads children to be fully engaged every step of the way and to retain their learning. As an additional benefit, the more that students experience Interactive Modeling, the better they become at very careful and skillful observing—and this carries over to other areas of their learning. For example, the second graders I described on pages 3–4 became more skilled at noticing and pointing out positive aspects of each other's work and key details in books they were reading after I started using Interactive Modeling regularly.

Students have a chance to practice and gain expertise. As many researchers have noted, practice is necessary to master any skill (see a sample of this research in Appendix C). The Interactive Modeling structure builds in time for all students to practice the behavior they just saw modeled. Such practice dramatically increases the likelihood that students will succeed in meeting the expectation for the behavior or skill.

Students receive immediate feedback. To truly learn, students need positive feedback about what they're doing well and what's leading to their success. They also need feedback about what they need to change or adjust. With Interactive Modeling, such feedback is built in. When student volunteers demonstrate the behavior (Step 4) and all students practice it (Step 6), the teacher provides meaningful feedback in the moment. This clear and immediate feedback helps cement the learning of the lesson.

Students who experience Interactive Modeling gain a much richer and deeper understanding of expectations than from conventional modeling. They encounter more success in meeting and even exceeding expectations and in developing positive behaviors and key academic and social skills. Classroom routines and procedures become automatic much more quickly, freeing up more time for learning. With Interactive Modeling, students gain foundational social and academic skills needed for school success.

How to Use This Book

In this book, you'll learn how to use Interactive Modeling effectively—what to teach, how to teach it, and what to avoid. Throughout the book, you'll find many practical examples, tips, and tools to make this powerful practice come alive.

You can use the book in different ways to best suit your needs. For example, if you have been struggling with a particular area (maybe students need to take better care of classroom materials), you can read the pertinent chapter (in this case, Chapter 4). Or, if you're getting ready to teach a particular skill, such as how to respond to the signal for quiet attention, you can zero in on a lesson covering that or a very similar skill. This book contains several sample lessons in each chapter, plus additional sample scripts in Appendix B.

Also, be sure to read Chapter 1. Its valuable global strategies and practical tips will help you succeed in using Interactive Modeling for any procedure, routine, or skill.

Regardless of whether you read straight through or skip around, I encourage you to use the Planning Guide and Timelines in Appendix A. These tools will help you prepare for and succeed with Interactive Modeling.

➤ Go to **www.responsiveclassroom.org/interactive-modeling** to see video clips of Interactive Modeling in action in real classrooms, or scan the code to go there now.

——— A Closing Thought ———

If you're a teacher, parent, coach, or anyone else who works with children, I hope you read on and give Interactive Modeling a try. I'm confident that you'll discover how powerful this technique can be for both you and the children you teach.

─── Chapter 1 ───

How to Do Interactive Modeling

When I was working on this book, my editor, Jim, and I were discussing our very different approaches to cooking. When I try cooking something new, I follow a recipe to the T. I don't start adapting it until I've reached a level of mastery. Jim's wife takes the same approach.

Jim never follows recipes exactly. He doesn't start with all the ingredients a recipe calls for, not even the first time he makes it. He uses the recipe as a guide, but changes the ingredients and instructions as he sees fit.

So I asked Jim, "Who do you consider a better cook—your wife or you?" "My wife," he answered without hesitation.

The Seven Steps of Interactive Modeling

1
Say what you will model and why.

2
Model the behavior.

3
Ask students what they noticed.

4
Invite one or more students to model.

5
Again, ask students what they noticed.

6
Have all students practice.

7
Provide feedback.

What does this have to do with Interactive Modeling? Although it may be tempting to vary the "recipe" of Interactive Modeling that's outlined in this chapter, I encourage you to stick to it as you begin using this teaching practice. Doing so will give you an idea of the power and flow of an Interactive Modeling lesson. It will also give you a chance to practice some of the tricky parts, such as being succinct in your opening statement, asking effective questions, and coaching with appropriate teacher language.

Once you've mastered the basic structure, you can decide if using an abbreviated format may be right for students at certain times. Chapter 7, pages 153–165, contains information about when it's best to use abbreviated Interactive Modeling formats, such as for reteaching a routine or skill after a long break.

As with other effective teaching practices, the simplicity of Interactive Modeling is a big part of what makes it so powerful. But although simple, each step has an important purpose—and understanding these purposes will help you get the most out of Interactive Modeling.

In this chapter, you'll get a closer look at the steps for Interactive Modeling and the purposes behind each. You'll also learn practical tips for doing Interactive Modeling well—and common mistakes to avoid.

Interactive Modeling in Action

The seven steps of Interactive Modeling are illustrated in the following example in which Ms. Green, a third grade teacher, shows students how to respond to a signal for quiet attention. Notice her precise use of language in each step.

10 minutes

How to Respond to the Signal for Quiet Attention

1 Say what you will model and why:

Ms. Green: "To help us stay safe and learn a lot, there will be times when I need to get your attention quickly. The way I'll signal for you to stop and listen is to ring this chime. I'm going to show you what to do when you hear it. Watch me and see what you notice."

2 Model the behavior:

Ms. Green starts writing. When she hears the chime, she carefully puts down the pencil, puts hands in lap, and looks at Juan (who agreed ahead of time to ring the chime).

3 Ask students what they noticed:

Ms. Green: "What did you see me do?"

Juan: "You looked at me."

Erika: "You put down your pencil."

Ms. Green: "How did I put it down?"

Erika: "You didn't slam it down."

Ms. Green: "So, what did I do?"

Erika: "You put it down gently."

Ms. Green: "What else did you notice?"

Kanye: "You were quiet."

Ms. Green: "Did you notice anything else I did with my hands besides put the pencil down?"

Devon: "Yes. You put them in your lap."

Ms. Green: "Why might that matter?"

Devon: "Because if we hold something, it can distract us."

4 Invite one or more students to model:

Ms. Green: "Could someone else show us how to respond to the chime the same way I did?" Sara volunteers. Ms. Green directs Sara to start writing something and then rings the chime. Sara responds just as Ms. Green did.

5 Again, ask students what they noticed:

Ms. Green leads the class in a discussion of what they noticed Sara doing.

6 Have all students practice:

Ms. Green: "Now everyone will practice. Your job is to respond to the chime just the way Sara and I did. This time, I'll do the watching and noticing." The children all start writing. When Ms. Green rings the chime, all the students put down their pencils, turn and look at her, and are quiet.

7 Provide feedback:

Ms. Green: "That was so fast! You were very careful with your pencils, and your quiet faces looking at me tell me you're ready to listen. We are going to have a great year of learning!"

Adapting Interactive Modeling Lessons

It's important to know that this or any other Interactive Modeling lesson in this book can easily be scaffolded, or adapted, to fit students' needs and abilities. For example, in the preceding lesson:

→ A teacher of younger children might have more students model individually before having the whole class practice.

→ A teacher of older children might use more sophisticated language in Step 1. For example: "Any group that's working together needs a signal to get everyone's attention. In our class, one of those signals will be the chime. I'll show you what to do when you hear it. See what you notice."

In each chapter that follows, you'll find brief notes about how you might tailor the sample Interactive Modeling lessons to best meet your students' specific needs and abilities. With a bit of practice, you'll have the skills you need to adapt the examples and create your own Interactive Modeling lessons.

—— Understanding the —— Seven Steps

1 Say what you will model and why.

WHY THIS STEP IS IMPORTANT:

Children are more likely to do something the way you taught it if they know the reason for it.

REMEMBER TO:

→ *Plan exactly what you'll say (you may want to write it out).* Doing so clarifies for you why the lesson matters and how to make it relevant to students.

→ *Keep it brief (a few short sentences at most).* Talking too much diminishes the power of the lesson.

→ *Use positive wording even when the lesson is in response to a problem.* For example, if students have been messy in the cafeteria, you might say, "Our rules say that we will take care of each other and our environment. I'm going to show you two ways to follow these rules in the cafeteria so that everyone has a great eating experience and we don't make extra work for the cafeteria staff. See what you notice about how I throw away my trash and stack my tray."

➤ *Refer to the class rules if you can.* For example, if you're modeling how students are to work independently when you're busy with a small group, you might say, "Our class rules say that we will take care of each other and do our best learning. When I'm with a small group and you're working at tables, that means you need to focus on your own learning. I'm going to show you one way to do that." Using the rules as an anchor communicates that you are not trying to control students but to support their needs as learners.

• •

The *Responsive Classroom* approach offers teachers practical ways to involve students in developing classroom rules. For more information, visit www.responsiveclassroom.org.

2 Model the behavior.

WHY THIS STEP IS IMPORTANT:

Hearing how we want them to do something isn't enough for most children. They need to see the behavior demonstrated so they'll have a mental image of *exactly* how to do it.

REMEMBER TO:

➤ *Practice the behavior yourself first.* Break it down into smaller pieces so you're sure to model it accurately. Practicing beforehand also means you won't take too long thinking while you model (and lose students' attention).

➤ *Stay silent as you model.* Unless talking is part of what you're teaching, don't narrate. Instead, let students notice the key aspects for themselves.

➤ *Avoid spontaneous additions.* One time, when teaching how to use the pencil sharpener, I hummed a little song as I modeled. Guess what the first student volunteer modeler did? Hummed the same exact tune! I was able to back up and recover, but the lesson would have been more powerful if I had modeled the specific behavior, no more and no less, in the first place.

3 Ask students what they noticed.

WHY THIS STEP IS IMPORTANT:

Students take in more and remember more if they notice key aspects of the expected behavior for themselves. Asking students what they noticed also enables you to quickly assess their understanding.

REMEMBER TO:

> ➥ *Use open-ended questions.* These are questions that require more than a *yes* or *no* and have no single right answer. You can simply ask, "What did you notice?" Or, to help students focus on a particular detail in your modeling, pose a more specific question, such as "What did you notice about what allowed both Becca and me to have a chance to talk?"

> ➥ *Ask a follow-up question if needed.* Do this if you want students to focus on why a certain behavior matters. For example: "Why does it matter that I looked at Becca when I talked with her?"

> ➥ *Accept any reasoned and relevant responses.* Be careful not to jump in too soon to ask about specific behaviors you want to highlight. Students will respond with enthusiasm when they believe you're truly interested in what *they* observed. If, after a few

---

The Think-Aloud Technique

Staying silent during Step 2 usually works best. But sometimes you'll want to make your thinking "visible" to students, such as when showing what self-control looks like or how to deal with strong emotions.

For example, to show students a way to calm down when they're upset, you might demonstrate taking deep breaths. As you do, you might say to them that you're thinking, "It's not really that big of a deal. I need to calm down before I say something I'll regret. I'll just take a few more breaths."

The Think-Aloud technique works well in these situations. For younger children, some teachers put a finger to their head while saying their thoughts aloud. Others hold up a drawing of a thought bubble on a craft stick. For older children, you can simply tell them that you're about to do a Think-Aloud.

responses, there's an important detail that students haven't named, use a prompting question to lead them toward it. For instance, in modeling how to walk from desks to the circle area, draw attention to the fact that you went there directly (without going to other areas) by asking, "What path did I take to get here?" or "How did I manage to get here so quickly?"

➤ *Emphasize what to do.* Often students name what the teacher was *not* doing. For instance, in a modeling of how to move a chair, a student might say, "You weren't swinging it around." Help the student say what you *were* doing instead. "So, what were my hands and arms doing?" For modeling to have the strongest effect, students need to create a positive image of what to do and say.

Reframing "You Didn'ts" to "You Dids"	
If a student says . . .	**You could ask . . .**
"You didn't run."	"So, how did I get there?"
"You didn't just flip through randomly."	"What did I do to figure out a good place to start?"
"You didn't just shove things in your desk."	"How did I make sure things went in the right place?"
"You didn't aim at his head."	"Where did I try to have the ball land?"
"You didn't let food go everywhere."	"What did I do to make sure that didn't happen?"
"You didn't yell or get rude."	"So, how did I talk to my partner?"

4 Invite one or more students to model.

WHY THIS STEP IS IMPORTANT:

Having students repeat your modeling gives the class multiple images of the behavior, which reinforces exactly how to do it.

REMEMBER TO:

➤ *Select students who will repeat your demonstration.* You may even want to practice with them beforehand. If you're unsure whether a student can repeat your modeling or sense that he or she may try something different or humorous, choose another volunteer.

➤ *Leave no doubt that students are to model exactly the way you did.* For example, say, "Who would like to demonstrate how to multiply fractions using the method I showed?" If your wording is too wide-open (such as "Who else can show us how to multiply fractions?"), the volunteer may model a different way. Although you might want that at other times, during Interactive Modeling the goal is to show one specific way to do something.

About Student Modelers

Although you should choose students you feel will model the behavior successfully, avoid using the same students as modelers again and again. Over time, and with your support, all students can successfully model in one lesson or another. For the greatest impact, use Interactive Modeling inclusively.

5 Again, ask students what they noticed.

WHY THIS STEP IS IMPORTANT:

This further reinforces the specific details of the behavior and allows you to quickly reassess students' understanding.

REMEMBER TO:

➤ *Repeat Steps 4 and 5 for somewhat challenging behaviors.* Consider students' developmental needs and abilities when deciding whether to do so. Older students sometimes need only one or two demonstrations, whereas younger students may need more.

6 Have all students practice.

WHY THIS STEP IS IMPORTANT:

Practice is critical to the mastering of any skill, routine, or procedure.

REMEMBER TO:

➤ *Spread out this practice if needed.* Sometimes you'll need to do this step later instead of having the whole class practice immediately after Step 5. For example, while all students can quickly and easily practice sitting on the carpet and showing attention, giving all students a turn at practicing how to save a document on the computer would likely take too long. In cases like this, have a few students practice at different times throughout a period or day so that you can watch.

➤ *Focus on progress, not perfection.* Students may make mistakes, which is a natural part of any practice—whether an academic, social, or other skill.

7 Provide feedback.

WHY THIS STEP IS IMPORTANT:

Much as players in sports depend upon feedback from coaches, students need feedback from you as they practice during a modeling lesson if they're going to truly learn a new skill.

REMEMBER TO:

➤ *Name the specific, positive actions you notice.* For example, if students are learning how to shake hands, you might say: "Almost everyone was shaking hands in a firm but gentle way with both palms touching. You shook only a few times and made eye contact."

➤ *Redirect students respectfully but clearly.* For example, if students do not follow your model of how to shake hands, you might say, "Hold on, Julie and Jemella, remember that your hands need to go all the way together so that your palms are touching. Show what that looks like."

➤ *Invite students to reflect on how they're doing.* You can ask for reflections during this last step of the modeling lesson or as informal check-ins later in the day. These reflections reinforce the Interactive Modeling lesson and hone students' critical thinking skills, such as evaluating and synthesizing.

Sample Reflective Questions to Ask Students	
If students are learning to . . .	**You could ask them . . .**
Move chairs	"How did we do with moving our chairs safely and efficiently?"
Give compliments	"What did we do well when we gave each other compliments?"
Do Internet searches	"What are some things that helped us do Internet searches successfully?"

➤ *Provide meaningful feedback to students.*

- **Name concrete behaviors.** For example: "I saw everyone greeting partners with a friendly face, eye contact, and a warm tone of voice."

- **Use a warm, professional tone.** Avoid sarcasm or gushing.

- **Avoid using words of personal approval,** such as "I like" or "I love." Instead, say "I noticed," "I heard," and "I saw."

• •

To learn more about giving effective feedback and other aspects of positive teacher language, go to www.responsiveclassroom.org.

Strategies for Success

✳

Take Time to Plan and Reflect

Interactive Modeling looks so straightforward that it may be tempting to "wing it." Don't give in to that temptation! Plan each lesson by thinking through what you will do and say (and what the children might do and say as well). For more complicated behaviors or routines, you may even want to practice by yourself or with a colleague.

Also think about what could go wrong or what students might misunderstand and how you can keep things on track, especially when student volunteers model (Step 4) and when the whole class practices (Step 6). In the chapters that follow, you'll learn how other teachers anticipate and plan around potential challenges.

Start Small

When you're just starting out using Interactive Modeling, consider which behaviors, procedures, and skills will help students be successful in their learning throughout the school year. Then, focus on just one or two of them to teach using Interactive Modeling. You might choose to start with what to do when you signal for quiet attention or how you expect students to line up when leaving the classroom.

Repeat these first lessons until both you and students are successful before using Interactive Modeling to teach other behaviors and routines. This way, both you and students can gain confidence and expertise with this teaching technique, which will better ensure that everyone can build upon their early successes.

Keep the Lesson Moving

Interactive Modeling lessons work best at a quick pace. Plan ahead so that you introduce and carry out the lesson efficiently. When you call on students to name what they noticed, stop after the key points have been raised. You needn't call on every single child. Keep the lesson moving by keeping it balanced between doing and listening.

Model Only the "Right" Way to Do Something

The power of Interactive Modeling largely comes from the positive images students form by seeing behaviors modeled correctly and repeatedly. So it's best not to show the "wrong" way to do certain behaviors. As I noted in the Introduction, modeling how not to do something confuses students because they form two (or more) competing mental images. Then, when you want them to perform a task, they may easily pull up the wrong image. For instance, think about how you teach academics. As my colleague Sarah Fillion points out, children don't learn to read by being taught *how not* to read. We want students to see and learn *how to* meet expectations.

Post Reminders for Challenging Behaviors

When behaviors require multiple steps, or when students are struggling with a behavior, support your Interactive Modeling lesson with a visual reminder. For instance, if you have modeled over several lessons how to do the many steps of the dismissal routine (organize desk, get homework folder, pack up backpack, and

Interactive Modeling or Role-Playing?

When it's important that students do something in one specific way, Interactive Modeling is usually the most effective technique to use. However, sometimes you may want children to have choices of what to do and build a repertoire of acceptable responses. To teach multiple ways to respond in a given situation, try the *Responsive Classroom* strategy of role-play.

To illustrate the difference, consider how to teach children what to do if they get "stuck" during independent work time without interrupting a teacher's work with a small group. Some teachers want students to do only one thing, such as read quietly until they have a free moment. So these teachers would use Interactive Modeling to show students exactly what to do. Other teachers might want students to have a set of options if they get stuck. They would use role-play to explore those options with students.

Teachers might also use role-play to build a repertoire of social and academic skills, such as by teaching students ways to approach someone to play with at recess and how to give respectful feedback on another student's writing.

For more on the *Responsive Classroom* approach to role-play, visit www.responsiveclassroom.org.

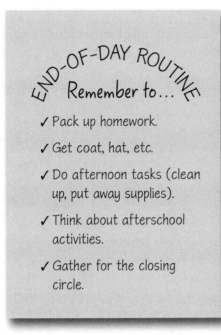

Sample End-of-Day Anchor Chart

so on), display an anchor chart or another visual reminder of the routine. One of my colleagues modeled how to organize cubby spaces and then took a photo of a "model cubby" to post above the cubbies. Another teacher has students make the visual reminders for themselves.

Remember the Goal of the Behaviors You're Teaching

Stay focused on the essentials in the behaviors you model. For example, the main goal of using a silent signal is to ensure that students can quickly focus their attention on you. As the class is practicing this response, recognize when students have given you their attention and move forward to bring the lesson to completion. Do so even if one or two children are a bit squirmy (but paying attention) or even if you have a student who has a hard time making eye contact in general (but who you know from other signs is paying attention).

Also avoid pointing out behaviors that were not part of your Interactive Modeling. For instance, if you were only modeling how to come quietly to the rug, don't choose that moment to point out that folders weren't (or were) put away neatly.

Reinforce Students' Success . . . Often!

In the days immediately following an Interactive Modeling lesson and periodically throughout the year, remind yourself to reinforce students' successes in meeting expectations. With so much going on each day, it's easy to forget to do so. We may think, "They all made the transition from my mini-lesson to independent work so smoothly. That will give me a few extra minutes with the small group." But when we fail to reinforce students' successes, they may feel that we really don't care about behaviors and expectations. Take the time—and it need only be a few seconds—to notice and comment specifically when students are doing what you showed them. For a transition behavior, you might say, "You made that transition so smoothly—I couldn't even hear you. I can't wait to see what you write now that you are so focused."

Be Alert to When Behavior Starts to Go Off Track

Rarely is one lesson all students need. Sometimes they forget the expectations; often they just need more practice. Hold students to your expectations by noticing when behaviors first go off track, rather than waiting until they're problematic. For example, if you modeled the appropriate volume level for independent work, step in and remind students of that level the minute they start to go over it. If you wait until they're too loud, they'll have a much harder time modulating themselves.

By intervening early, you give students a better chance to successfully meet expectations and reinforce the power of your words and lessons. If you find yourself reminding too many students or doing so frequently, you may need to remodel the expected behavior.

Look for Cooperation, Not Absolute Compliance

Intervening early is not the same as being rigid. In the effort to establish and hold students to high expectations, some teachers demand perfection—for instance, that children stand in line without fidgeting, face forward, and be perfectly still while the teacher gives directions. Or, they insist that children make transitions with robot-like efficiency. Such demands for perfection won't lead to the calm, safe, learning-conducive atmosphere that we want and students need. Students can still be safe in line and hear what we're saying even when they're not perfectly still. Transitions can be smooth and efficient while having a calm, relaxed feel.

Being too rigid in expectations also sets up a detrimental dynamic between students and teachers. Students may feel that we're trying to control them. Many will rebel, sometimes when we're looking but more often when they

know we're not. Interactive Modeling is designed to encourage cooperation, not dronelike compliance.

We do need to have high expectations, but tempered with a good dose of realism, knowledge of what students are capable of at this stage in their development, and an understanding of the particular group of children in front of us. For example, when I use Interactive Modeling to show children how to turn and talk with a partner, I teach them to stay on the topic assigned. But I know it's natural for children (and adults) to occasionally detour from that topic. So I don't immediately intervene for every detour because I also know that most conversations quickly return to the main topic.

Think About Your Expectations

At times, our missteps lie in *what* we are teaching, not *how* we are teaching it. If your students are having difficulty with a particular behavior, it might be that your expectations for them are too high or not developmentally appropriate. For instance, I could do an Interactive Modeling lesson about how to work in a cooperative group of four with second graders, but even with careful teaching, they might still struggle with this skill because second graders often do better working alone or in pairs.

Give Extra Support to Those Who Need It

Having realistic expectations also means giving special supports to those children who need them, just as we do for those who need extra support in math or reading. If I modeled how to show respectful disagreement when working on a project, but I know that two students struggle with phrasing things diplomatically and using an appropriate tone of voice, it would be unrealistic to think that they are going to perfect the skill of respectfully disagreeing right away.

So I need to find ways to support those struggling students. For example, I might do a little more private modeling and practice with them before sending them to work on a project. Or I might make them my partners and have them practice expressing disagreement to me. I might also give them sentence starters to use as they begin working with "real" partners. In addition to providing extra supports, it's also helpful to have some empathy for children who are struggling. Usually their struggles result from multiple causes that have nothing to do with us. To learn more about reteaching and helping students who are struggling, see Chapter 7, starting on page 153.

And Have Fun!

Children learn and retain more when they're enjoying themselves, so try to infuse joy and fun into Interactive Modeling whenever you can. If you're working on walking quietly in line from one classroom area to another, give students something to think about as they practice. They could count by twos until they reach the destination, try to find words that start with a certain letter or letter combination on displays, look for particular shapes in the environment, or solve a challenging riddle or mental puzzle.

If many or all students—or you—mess up during a modeling lesson, use humor to start over. Sometimes I would say to a class of second graders, "Good thing this is a movie. We can just try that scene again!"

FAQs From Classroom Teachers

✳

➤ How do you decide what to do an Interactive Modeling lesson on?

Before the school year even starts, I often encourage teachers to brainstorm a list of procedures, routines, and skills that they want students to do in one particular way. Brainstorming with a colleague can be helpful. You may also want to use some of the lists and ideas in this book to jumpstart your brainstorming, including the Timelines on pages 171–173. Then, prioritize which procedures, routines, and skills are most essential and should be taught on the first day of school, which ones can wait, and so forth.

Sometimes, despite such careful planning, you may need to do additional Interactive Modeling lessons that you didn't foresee the need for. For example, one year entering the classroom at the start of school was proving very difficult for a class of kindergartners, with a lot of jostling and rough play. This was not something that the teacher expected. So she asked a colleague to observe the kindergartners' entrance one morning. After they discussed what the colleague noticed, the kindergarten teacher made a plan for exactly what she wanted students to do when they entered and she crafted an Interactive Modeling lesson to teach those expectations.

➤ During the student volunteer modeling (Step 4), what do I do if the student volunteer does not follow my modeling?

Stay calm and assume that the student had the best intentions. Perhaps he or she simply missed some key piece of your modeling. Let the student know that he or she will have a chance to practice again. In the meantime, call upon another volunteer: "Stop, Alli. I want to make sure everyone sees how to _____ exactly the way I showed. Have a seat for a second. You'll get to try again in a few minutes. Kiri, come give it a try." Or you may decide you need to remodel the behavior yourself.

➤ **What if during the whole-class practice phase (Step 6), most students do not follow the modeling?**

Sometimes this will happen. Start by asking yourself why: Did a few students get off track and take the other students with them? Were the modelings not as clear as they needed to be? Were students not taking their practice seriously because they didn't understand why it mattered? Or was the behavior more challenging for students than you had anticipated?

If you are fairly certain students "got it" but were just carried away with something silly or a higher than ordinary energy level, help them quickly regroup. Remember that a little humor or playfulness helps. You might say something like: "Oops, freeze. I know you can move to your seats the way I just showed. I'm going to close my eyes. When I open them, I bet I'll see you doing it." If you think the reason may lie in a weak part of your lesson, redo the modeling right away if you can do so quickly, or do it at a later time.

Keep in mind that students may also simply need more practice. If so, point out and reinforce the positives in their first attempt and then set a goal for the next practice time. For example: "At the beginning, I saw you trying to put the pattern blocks in the containers carefully and quietly. It was quiet for about fifteen seconds. Then, the noise started to rise, and we got a little carried away. I bet next time we can try for quiet cleanup for twenty-five seconds!"

➤ **How does Interactive Modeling work with students who are still learning English or have difficulty communicating verbally?**

In one school where I taught, many of the kindergartners had a hard time expressing their ideas, either because English was their second language or their vocabularies and expressive skills were just not well developed. I modified my Interactive Modeling by allowing students to show me what they saw me do in Step 3, and I narrated what they showed me. For instance, when I modeled how to respond to the chime and asked what they noticed, one student made her eyes bigger and stared at me. I responded, "Oh, you saw me really looking at the teacher and paying attention." She nodded and smiled in agreement. Sometimes, I would follow up and say, "Let's all show what that looks like," before moving on to what another student noticed.

➤ Do you use Interactive Modeling to teach all procedures and classroom behaviors? If so, is Interactive Modeling all you do for the first few days of school?

Interactive Modeling is useful to teach any procedure, behavior, or skill that students need to do in a particular way over and over again. So, yes, I would use it quite a bit during the first few days of school. But remember, each lesson should be fairly short. In general, I try to intersperse these lessons with other activities during the first few days of school.

➤ Don't students get bored with the format of Interactive Modeling lessons? Does its effectiveness wear off?

I find that the more I use Interactive Modeling, the better students and I become at it and the more we all enjoy it. I work at asking questions that are likely to engage students, such as "Why might it be important to do _____?" during Steps 3 and 5. And most students become quite enthralled with their job as "noticers," or observers. Also, if you remember to keep the pace quick, maintain a positive tone, and include a little fun whenever you can, Interactive Modeling will be even more engaging for everyone.

——— A Closing Thought ———

When you explicitly teach students through well-paced Interactive Modeling lessons, they'll be much more likely to meet expectations and build skills. And keep in mind that you can often use a well-planned Interactive Modeling lesson again—and for years to come.

Points to Remember

✳

→ *Understand why each of the seven steps is important.*

→ *Connect the modeling to classroom rules and learning goals.*

→ *Prioritize and start small.* Start with simpler routines and skills that children need right away and build up to those that are more complex.

→ *Model exactly how you want students to do a skill or routine.* Interactive Modeling works best for routines and skills that need to be done one way and when you model that one way only.

→ *Keep the lesson moving and the pace appropriate for your students.*

→ *Evaluate your expectations.* Reevaluate them if things change. Provide support to students who need it.

→ *Reinforce success often.* Focus on the positives you notice and the progress students are making.

• • • • • • • • • • • •

For more help creating effective Interactive Modeling lessons, use the Planning Guide and Timelines in Appendix A, pages 169–173.

Chapter 2

Routines and Interactive Modeling

Routines

Like many teachers, I went into the profession full of enthusiasm about teaching children how to read, add, and subtract. And, like many who have stayed in the profession, I have come to appreciate—and even love—the "other" things we have to teach: social skills, routines, and procedures. Of course academic subjects are important. Yet much of what will lead to successful academic outcomes for children is the attention we give to these "other" aspects of our day.

Routines that are well planned and taught through Interactive Modeling can make the difference between a classroom that runs smoothly and one that looks and feels chaotic. A recent experience illustrates what a difference using Interactive Modeling can make in establishing strong routines.

Not too long ago, I visited a fourth grade classroom that was too small for a permanent circle area. The teacher had found a way around this obstacle by developing a simple routine. When it was time for students to gather in a circle, they quickly and seamlessly moved their desks out of the way. The teacher and students then quickly gathered in a circle and focused on the activity at hand. When their circle business was concluded, they just as quickly moved the desks back. This routine was powerful enough to overcome the physical constraints of the classroom so that the teacher could teach the way he felt was best for students.

The behind-the-scenes work that made this routine successful was Interactive Modeling. When introducing this Interactive Modeling lesson, the teacher impressed upon students how important it would be for the class community to get this routine down and be able to do it quickly. "It's important for our class to be able to meet in a circle where we can see each other, care for each other, and do fun things together. To do that, we're going to have to learn how to move some desks out of the way quickly and safely. Do you think you can do this job in twenty seconds or less? I think you can."

He proceeded to break down each step of the process—moving the desks back, forming a circle, and then putting the desks back into place—and he taught each step through a separate Interactive Modeling lesson. The repeated modeling and practicing enabled students to master moving desks and forming a circle quickly and safely. With the routine firmly established, the teacher could easily meet with students in a circle as often as needed.

In this chapter, you'll learn effective strategies for using Interactive Modeling to plan and teach routines for whole-group work, lunch, recess, and more. (Note that arrival and dismissal procedures are discussed in Chapter 3.)

—— Routines and ——
Interactive Modeling

✳

Whole-Group Classroom Routines

Some of the most important routines to teach first are those for how to listen and pay attention during whole-group and instructional times. The clearer you can be about what you expect for these routines, the more smoothly discussions, class meetings, giving directions, and teaching the curriculum will go.

Think about which routines you want to model to help your students succeed with whole-group classroom learning. For example:

➤ Responding to the signal for quiet attention

➤ Where and how to sit

➤ Showing that you are listening

➤ Signaling a desire to speak during a discussion (such as when you have an idea while someone else is talking)

➤ Using a signal to show a connection to what someone is saying

➤ Chatting with a partner

➤ What to do if someone tries to talk to you during a lesson

➤ What to do if you need help

For an Interactive Modeling lesson on the signal for quiet attention, see Chapter 1, pages 13–14; for a script on listening, see Appendix B, page 175.

Independent Work Time Routines

Your students will undoubtedly spend a great deal of time during the school year working independently on various assignments, projects, and tasks. You want this time to be productive for everyone, and you may also want to use some of this time to meet—uninterrupted—with a small group or an individual student. However, working independently requires that students learn and master a wide range of skills.

Think about which routines you want to model with your students so they can be successful when working independently. For example:

→ Responding to the signal for quiet attention

→ Working in a given spot

→ Having a brief, quiet conversation

→ What to do if you struggle with the assignment (and how to ask for help)

→ Helping another classmate (how and when)

→ What to do if someone is bothering you

→ Where to put completed work (and what to do when you finish)

Independent work skills take awhile for students to master, so it's especially important to identify which skills students need to learn early in the year and which ones can wait until later.

Mrs. Kurland, a fifth grade teacher, decided to use Interactive Modeling with a "fish bowl" strategy to teach students how to stay in one's seat, focus on an assignment, and occasionally converse quietly about that assignment with tablemates. She set up a small table and four chairs in the center of the circle where she and several other students whom she'd prepped beforehand demonstrated the skills of independent work time. The other students sat in chairs around the table and observed the action in this "fish bowl." To see how Mrs. Kurland's Interactive Modeling lesson went, take a look at the example on the next page.

20–25 minutes

Working Independently

1 Say what you will model and why:

Mrs. Kurland: "Our goal for everyone this year is to do high-quality work. To reach that goal, your job is to work hard on your assignments and let other people do the same. Watch and see how Carlos, Eliza, Eduardo, and I do that as we work on our research."

2 Model the behavior:

Mrs. Kurland and the three students (coached beforehand) go to a table in the center of the circle and start working intently. After a short time, to show students that some talking is OK during this time, she turns to Carlos and quietly tells him one fact she read. He responds, "Wow, that's cool," also in a quiet voice. They both return to work.

3 Ask students what they noticed:

Mrs. Kurland: "What did you notice about how we took care of ourselves and each other?"

Lionel: "You were all reading your books."

Maryann: "You were all quiet."

Jillisa: "You didn't get up and wander around."

Mrs. Kurland: [*smiling*] "So what did we do?"

Jillisa: "You stayed in your seat."

Mrs. Kurland: "What difference does that make?"

Jillisa: "It's hard to get anything done if you keep getting up and down."

Mrs. Kurland: [*to make sure students noticed the talking*] "What did you notice about whether we talked or not?"

Lionel: "You did talk."

Mrs. Kurland: "What did we talk about?"

Lionel: "Your research."

Mrs. Kurland: "How long and how loud was our conversation?"

Maryann: "Very short and pretty quiet."

4 Invite one or more students to model:

Ms. Kurland chooses four students to demonstrate and asks two of them, Aiko and Mason, to have a quick, quiet conversation about something they read.

Mrs. Kurland: "Anna, Dominique, Aiko, and Mason are going to demonstrate how to focus on independent work. Watch and see what you notice."

5 Again, ask students what they noticed:

After a few minutes of their demonstration, Mrs. Kurland has the students return to their seats.

Mrs. Kurland: "What did you notice about the way they made the most of their independent work time?" Students point out the key behaviors, including the quiet, quick conversation Aiko and Mason had.

6 Have all students practice:

To help students succeed at this practice, Mrs. Kurland uses an engaging task (a survey about themselves).

Mrs. Kurland: "At your tables, there's a personal survey for you to complete. It will help us learn more about each other and practice what independent work looks like."

7 Provide feedback:

Mrs. Kurland: [*to reinforce initial success*] "I'm seeing everyone already focused on the survey. Your pencils are moving, and you're staying in your seats."

After a few minutes, she sees a few students chatting quietly and briefly as demonstrated.

Mrs. Kurland: [*to reinforce positive behaviors*] "You're having brief, quiet conversations and then getting back to work. That kind of focus will help us complete our work and learn a lot this year!"

One student who struggles with control gets a little loud and calls across to someone.

Mrs. Kurland: [*moving close to student*] "Emma, keep your voice down and talk only to people at your table. We'll have time to share with everyone at the end."

After about five minutes, another student who struggles with writing is getting restless. Mrs. Kurland knows this boy needs a movement break to be successful, so she quietly goes over to him and asks him to take a brief walk around the classroom to regain focus. The work time continues with a mix of reinforcement, reminding, and redirecting.

● ●

To adapt this lesson for younger students:

Break it up into separate lessons. First, model what focused, independent work looks like. Then, in a separate lesson, model how to interact with those working nearby.

Bathroom Routines

Wouldn't it be nice if you could just point out where the bathrooms are and let children take it from there? In reality, children need much more explicit guidance. Because bathroom procedures can vary greatly from one grade to the next and depend on factors such as bathroom locations, children need you to teach these routines during the first few days of school.

Think about which routines you want to model with your students so they can be successful when using the bathroom. For example:

- ➤ When students may go and how many may go at the same time

- ➤ How to show they need to go and show they have returned, such as by using a card system or a sign-out/sign-in system

- ➤ What to do while in the bathroom (toilet paper use, flushing, washing hands, cleaning up around sink, trash disposal)

- ➤ What to do if there's a mechanical problem (the toilet won't flush, no toilet paper)

- ➤ How to take care of themselves and others in the bathroom, and on the way to and from the bathroom (such as when they see a friend or if someone is being unkind)

For an Interactive Modeling script on using the bathroom, see Appendix B, page 182.

Cafeteria Routines

Cafeteria events can have a major impact on the rest of the day. If students have the skills to enjoy a healthy lunch, they'll be more energized to learn. If they have the skills to interact positively with peers, those relationships can carry over to make all parts of school happier and more productive.

Of course, the opposite is also true. If students are too rowdy, they may return to class with lots of unfocused energy. And negative encounters with classmates can have long-lasting effects that derail even the best academic lesson plan. It's worth reflecting on what students need to know for success in the cafeteria and how you will teach those skills. For example:

- Getting a tray, utensils, and napkins and going through the food line

- Sincerely thanking cafeteria staff

- Paying or using a ticket system

- Staying in one seat, using appropriate table manners, and talking at a reasonable volume

- Responding to the signal for quiet attention

- Signaling a need to go to the bathroom

- Handling spills

- Returning and stacking tray, getting rid of trash, and cleaning table or area

- Lining up for dismissal

- What to do while waiting in line, such as playing quiet hand games

To learn how Mr. O'Grady, a second grade teacher, taught students how lunch should look and sound, read the example that follows.

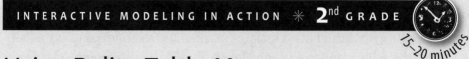

INTERACTIVE MODELING IN ACTION ✳ **2**nd GRADE

15–20 minutes

Using Polite Table Manners in the Cafeteria

1 Say what you will model and why:

Mr. O'Grady begins his lesson in the classroom. Later, he will hold lessons in the cafeteria.

Mr. O'Grady: "Lunchtime needs to be friendly and safe. One way to have that kind of lunchtime is to use polite table manners. Turn your body so you can see the blue table. Watch and see what I say and do."

2 Model the behavior:

Mr. O'Grady sits at the table with two stuffed animals (instead of student volunteers) and a prepared snack. He takes a bite and begins demonstratively chewing with his mouth closed.

Mr. O'Grady: [*swallowing his food and then speaking to the animals*] "Rufus, what do you like to do after school? . . . Oh, I love to play basketball, too."

He takes another bite of snack and pretends that "Rufus" has asked him a question.

Mr. O'Grady: [*holding up a finger until finished chewing*] "Sorry, I wanted to wait until I finished. You asked what kinds of animals I like. Well, I like all animals, but especially dogs like you."

3 Ask students what they noticed:

Mr. O'Grady: "What did you notice about how I tried to make lunch friendly and safe for everyone at my table?"

Nora: "You didn't talk with your mouth full."

Mr. O'Grady: [*following up*] "Well then, what did I do?"

Jeremy: "You chewed."

Mr. O'Grady: "How did I chew?"

Saundra: "With your mouth closed."

Mr. O'Grady: "Why do you think I chew with my mouth closed and finish chewing before I talk?"

Remi: "Sometimes, food comes flying out if you talk and chew at the same time."

Mr. O'Grady: [*summing up*] "So to make sure we don't gross anyone out and keep everyone safe, we'll chew with our mouths closed and talk only when we're not chewing." [*pausing*] "What did you notice about the conversation Rufus and I had?"

Felicia: "It was nice."

Mr. O'Grady: [*following up*] "What was nice about it? What did we talk about?"

Nora: "You talked about what you do after school and what kind of animals you like."

Mr. O'Grady: [*summing up*] "Lunch is a great time to get to know each other, so animals and what you like to do after school are good things to talk about." [*pausing*] "Where was I when I ate lunch?"

Jeremy: [*hesitantly*] "At your table?"

Mr. O'Grady: [*following up*] "Where at my table?"

Felicia: "In your chair."

Mr. O'Grady: [*summing up*] "Yes, we stay in our seats at lunch to make sure we are all safe."

4 Invite one or more students to model:

Mr. O'Grady: "Who can show us how to eat lunch the same way I did?" Mr. O'Grady invites Caylee and Owen to sit with him at the table and serves them a snack.

Mr. O'Grady: "Watch and see what you notice about how we use polite manners and learn more about each other at lunch." He engages the two in brief conversations about their favorite movies.

5 Again, ask students what they noticed:

Mr. O'Grady: [*concerned that the class has been sitting too long*] "Stand up and share with a partner what you noticed about how we kept lunchtime friendly and safe." After a few minutes, he calls on several students to report the key aspects that they talked about.

6 Have all students practice:

Mr. O'Grady: "Now we're all going to practice. I have some trail mix for each of you. I'm going to watch you practice being friendly and safe and taking care of those around you while you eat."

7 Provide feedback:

Mr. O'Grady: [*to reinforce initial success*] "Lots of you are remembering to keep your mouths closed while you chew, and I hear many happy conversations. We're off to a good start with lunch."

Mr. O'Grady sees one student eating messily. He makes a mental note to keep an eye on him, knowing that sloppy table manners can be off-putting to others and even lead to social isolation.

Mr. O'Grady lists some of the conversation topics he hears. Later, the class will add more ideas to the list. After a few more minutes, he asks students to come to the rug. He will teach cleanup a bit later. For now, he wants to capitalize on the successes in the room.

Mr. O'Grady: "What did you notice those at your table doing to make lunch safe and friendly?"

• •

To adapt this lesson for younger students:

Begin with a simple lesson on staying in one spot, keeping hands to oneself, and focusing on eating. After a week or so, model how to talk politely with tablemates while eating. Still later, model how to have an interesting, open-topic conversation at lunch.

• •

To adapt this lesson for older students:

Ask what they already know about taking care of each other at lunch. Then call on a small group to model with you what they point out and any additional behaviors you want to show.

Recess Routines

Like lunch, recess can be a wonderfully energizing time of the day. A positive recess enables children to feel refreshed and included socially—and these feelings carry over to academics. But for children to enjoy success at recess, they need to master many skills.

Think about which routines you want to model with your students so they can be successful at recess. For example:

➝ Knowing the boundaries of the playground areas (see page 94 in Chapter 4 for information on modeling the safe use of playground equipment)

➝ Circling up to hear instructions or feedback

➝ Choosing appropriate activities and games to play

➝ Safe running, safe tagging, and other rules

➝ What to do if they're hurt

➝ How to help someone else who is hurt

➝ Getting an adult's attention

➝ Inviting someone to play

➝ Joining in play that's already begun

➤ Getting permission to go to the bathroom

➤ Responding to the end-of-recess signal

For an Interactive Modeling script on quickly circling up at recess, see Appendix B, page 183.

Emergency Routines

Interactive Modeling is a powerful strategy for teaching children what to do in case of an emergency. We want students to have a clear mental picture of exactly what they are supposed to do, whether for a schoolwide emergency (such as a fire, earthquake, tornado, or lockdown) or for a classroom accident (such as someone throwing up or having a bathroom incident).

In an emergency, children need to know how to take care of themselves and their classmates. Some emergency skills that children should know include:

➤ Signals for "it's an emergency" (both a verbal and a nonverbal signal)

➤ What to do if they're working independently

➤ What to do if they're in the circle or another whole-group setting

➤ How to line up and exit the classroom

➤ What to do for each specific type of emergency

Here's how Mrs. LaRue, a first grade teacher, taught students what to do in case of a classroom accident:

15 minutes

Going to Your Seat in Case of a Classroom Accident

1 Say what you will model and why:

Mrs. LaRue: [*checking on their prior experiences*] "Today we're going to talk about how to take care of each other when there's an accident in our classroom. Thumbs up if you or someone you know has ever had a bloody nose at school." [*pauses to acknowledge students with thumbs up*] "Thumbs up if you or someone you know has ever thrown up at school." [*pauses again*]

Mrs. LaRue: "Sometimes accidents like these happen. Also, sometimes Ms. Vazquez [the principal] or another adult may have to interrupt us. When we have an accident or a big interruption, I'll need to help whoever needs me. You will need to stay safe and keep learning, so we need a way to take care of each other. Watch what I say and do to signal that it's an emergency." Mrs. LaRue says, "SOS," and opens her hand, closes it, and opens it again.

Mrs. LaRue: "Now I'm going to show you what to do when you see and hear that 'SOS' signal. Cameron, you be me and give the 'SOS' signal. Everyone else, watch what I do."

2 Model the behavior:

Cameron says "SOS" and makes the hand motions. Mrs. LaRue leaves the circle, goes straight to a desk, gets a book out of a book bag, and starts reading.

3 Ask students what they noticed:

Mrs. LaRue: "What did I do so that the 'teacher' could take care of the accident?"

Tito: "You went back to your desk."

Mrs. LaRue: [*following up*] "How did I go back?"

Dawn: "You didn't run."

Mrs. LaRue: [*following up*] "What did I do?"

Taylor: "You walked."

Mrs. LaRue: "How fast did I go?"

William: "You went medium."

Mrs. LaRue: "And what was my voice doing on my way there?"

Lucia: "Nothing."

Mrs. LaRue: [*prompting*] "What if you really want to know what the accident is and I can't tell you. What should your voice do then?"

Jair: "Nothing. Stay quiet."

Mrs. LaRue: "That's right. When an accident happens, I might not have time to explain what it is. You'll still need to go back to your desk quietly. And now, think about what I did when I got to my desk. What did I do to take care of myself and others during the accident?"

Tito: "You read a book from your book bag."

Mrs. LaRue: "Yes. You read from your book bags when it's a classroom accident or interruption."

4 Invite one or more students to model:

Mrs. LaRue: "Who would like to show us how to take care of each other during a classroom accident?" Amanda volunteers. Upon Mrs. LaRue's SOS signal, Amanda goes straight back to her desk and gets a book out of her book bag.

5 Again, ask students what they noticed:

Mrs. LaRue: "What did you see Amanda do that would help me to take care of an accident?" Students point out that Amanda immediately got up, went to her desk, and got a book out to read.

Mrs. LaRue: [*following up*] "What did Amanda do to find out what the accident was?"

Khalil: "Nothing. She stayed quiet."

Mrs. LaRue: [*increasing the complexity*] "Let's watch a few people respond to the 'SOS' signal all at once. Watch and see how they take care of each other and allow me to deal with the accident." Mrs. LaRue repeats Steps 4 and 5 with three student modelers.

6 Have all students practice:

Mrs. LaRue: "Now we're all going to practice. I'll watch and see how you take care of each other and the person who had an accident."

7 Provide feedback:

Although a few students are looking around, most are looking at their books. Mrs. LaRue decides to focus on the positives and students' initial successes.

Mrs. LaRue: "Wow! You were so careful, safe, and fast. It only took you eight seconds to get to your desks and have books out. Everyone was quiet and looked out for each other. If it were a real emergency, I would definitely be able to take care of whoever needed me!"

• •

To adapt this lesson for older students:

Consider beginning with an Interactive Modeling lesson on emergencies such as lockdown procedures, severe weather, or fire drills. Then, during an Interactive Modeling lesson on independent work time, cover how to stay focused when there are classroom interruptions, such as a student getting sick.

Tips for Success With Routines

Plan the routine carefully.

Planning out how a routine will look, sound, and feel is as important as planning out any other lesson or aspect of classroom life. Use the Planning Guide in Appendix A, pages 169–170, to help you focus on the key aspects of the routine you want to teach and how you will teach each step.

Consult colleagues.

Too often as teachers, we work in isolation and try to figure out how to do things completely on our own. Instead, seek out colleagues to talk through routines, especially those colleagues whose classes always seem to do quite well with routines. Chat with them to find out how they set up these routines and then adapt their ideas so you can effectively meet the needs of your class. For greater efficiency and consistency, share plans among teachers and other staff.

Break routines into manageable steps.

Most routines have multiple steps, so be sure to picture these or actually try them out yourself. Depending upon the age of the students you teach and what you know about them, you may want to teach the steps all at once or through separate Interactive Modeling lessons. For instance, in teaching a cafeteria routine, teachers of older students might teach all these steps in one lesson: getting your tray and utensils, making food selections, paying for food, and going to one's table. Those who teach younger students might teach each step separately.

Avoid trying to teach all routines at once.

It's impossible to teach all the routines your students will need to know on the first day (or even during the first week) of school. Consider which routines to teach first for initial success. As students master these, build up from there. For instance, when teaching recess routines to second graders, on the first day of school I modeled three key routines—circling up to hear directions, playing safely and with kindness, and lining up safely at the end of recess. Then, in the days that followed, I gradually added Interactive Modeling lessons for playing other games safely, helping if someone got hurt, signaling the need to go to the bathroom, and cleaning up. See the timeline below to learn how I spread out this teaching during the first three weeks of school.

Teaching Recess Routines Sample Timeline			
First day of school	**First week**	**Second week**	**Third week**
Circling up, playing safely, lining up (separately and in combination).	Early in the week: tag rules (safe tagging, taggers' choice, and so on). Middle of week: what to do if someone gets hurt, how to signal to a teacher the need to use the bathroom. Later in week: safe use of permanent playground equipment (slide, swing, climbing apparatus).	Safe use and storage of other recess equipment and supplies (Hula-hoops, bubbles, jump ropes, etc.).	Safe use and storage of indoor recess items (unless bad weather required earlier teaching).

For sample timelines to help you plan Interactive Modeling lessons throughout the school year, see Appendix A, pages 171–173.

Give children a sense of timing and pacing expectations.

Be sure to share your expectations for timing and pacing with students in your Interactive Modeling. For instance, if you're modeling how to walk through the cafeteria line, use a prompting question to draw students' attention to your walking pace if they do not comment on it themselves.

With older students, I might ask, "About how long did it take me to make my way through the line?" For younger students, I might ask, "What did you notice about how fast I went?" Similarly, if you're modeling how lunch cleanup should look, make sure that your lesson occurs at the same pace you want children to use. Again, call their attention to this pace if they do not notice it on their own.

Tell students the reason for the routine.

Whenever possible, ground your teaching of routines in classroom rules. For example, when teaching students a signal for showing a connection to what someone is saying, you might say, "Our rules say that we'll take care of and listen to each other. One way to do that when others are speaking is to show them a sign if you have a connection to something they're saying. Watch and see what that looks like."

It's true that when you create initial routines with students in the first week or so of school, you probably won't have those classroom rules in place. However, you still need to teach routines, so what do you do? You can base the routines on the aspirations you have for the upcoming year and the kind of community you want the class to form. For example:

- ➤ "I expect this classroom to be a place where everyone feels safe and cared for, so I'm going to show you _____."

- ➤ "We all need to take care of our own learning and other people's learning, so I'm going to demonstrate _____."

- ➤ "Everyone in this room has a right to feel safe. To make sure we each feel that way, we need to _____."

Once you teach a routine, stick to it.

Teachers who constantly change routines (or modify expectations each time) invite confusion and testing from students. Plan your routines in detail and be clear about your expectations. Then be firm in holding yourself and students to those standards, such as by reteaching if you notice a student or students struggling a bit. For more on reteaching, see the next page.

Build consistency across classrooms with your colleagues.

Without meaning to, we often make students learn different ways to do a similar task in other classrooms or areas. Although many students do manage to master different teachers' expectations and routines, doing so takes more mental energy—brainpower that they could be using for academic learning. And some students, unfortunately, constantly struggle as they try to master differing expectations and routines.

To the extent you can, collaborate with your colleagues, including special area teachers with whom you share students, and plan for consistent routines. For instance, could you all agree on:

- One or two common signals for quiet attention?

- How students should volunteer to speak in a classroom discussion?

- What the noise level should be in hallways or during transitions?

The more consistent we teachers can make routines, the more likely that our students will do them automatically. In addition, by collaborating with colleagues, you can plan Interactive Modeling lessons together and share them.

Reteach routines as needed.

The ultimate goal of modeling and practicing routines is to have them become automatic. However, it's unrealistic to expect all children to reach this "automaticity" after just one modeling session. Even after routines are well established, students may forget or certain situations may trip them up.

At the first sign that students are forgetting some key aspects of a routine, reteach that routine. If you wait until they've gone completely off track, correcting their missteps will be harder. For instance, a week or so after modeling how to wait and not interrupt you while you work with another student during independent work time, you notice that two students are regularly coming to you with questions. At that point, you might want to reteach them (and perhaps the whole class) the strategies you modeled for what do while waiting. For more on reteaching, see Chapter 7, starting on page 153.

Reinforce success.

One way to help routines stick and avoid "slippage" is to be vigilant in seeing and commenting on students' successes. For example, take a few minutes after recess to notice what students did well. When children line up on time, you might say, "Wow, you were having so much fun at recess, but you all came so fast at the signal. You are showing respect for everyone's learning time when you respond like that." Paying attention to success with routines—and why that success benefits the community—will help students strengthen positive behaviors and preserve more time for learning in the long run.

—— A Closing Thought ——

When children master the routines of their day and develop positive habits, they'll be better prepared for learning—and have more time for it. Interactive Modeling is an effective technique for teaching students these essential routines for school success.

Points to Remember

✳

➤ *List the routines that your students will need for success.*

➤ *Reflect on why the routine is important for students.* Connect each routine to classroom rules and learning goals.

➤ *Evaluate each routine.* Think about what may be challenging for students, identify their strengths, nd consider their developmental characteristics.

➤ *Break each routine down into small steps.* Based on students' needs and abilities, teach steps separately, in chunks, or all at once.

➤ *Plan Interactive Modeling lessons for each routine.* Prioritize the best times to teach each routine. Spread out this teaching, as needed.

➤ *Be consistent.* Once you teach a routine, stick with it. Reteach if needed.

➤ *Reinforce success.* Watch for student's successes (big and small). Use positive teacher language to reinforce these successes and to provide specific feedback.

• • • • • • • • • • • •

For more help using Interactive Modeling with routines, use the Planning Guide and Timelines in Appendix A, pages 169–173.

Chapter 3

Why Transitions Are Challenging

59

Transitions and Interactive Modeling

Tips for Success With Transitions

76

Points to Remember

81

Transitions

Smooth transitions can make all the difference between positive or negative learning experiences, effective or ineffective lessons, and pleasant or stressful social interactions. Yet transitions are some of the most challenging moments of a school day—both for teachers and for students.

In my early years of teaching, I taught what I thought were powerful mini-lessons about key aspects of the writer's craft. But when I sent the second graders back to practice their writing, many of them took a long time to get started. It was amazing to see them get sidetracked so easily! Some stopped to chat with peers, others slowly gathered their writing notebooks, and most got up to sharpen (and resharpen) pencils. By the time students had settled in to write, way too many had forgotten the point of the mini-lesson or their assignment.

I realized that I needed to give as much attention to teaching the transition from mini-lesson to independent writing time as to the mini-lesson itself. I began by thinking through the children's stumbling blocks and made a plan for addressing them:

➤ From a developmental perspective, I knew that children needed a social release after the mini-lesson and before they started writing.

➤ I decided to do an Interactive Modeling lesson on how to "turn and talk" with a partner about a writing plan, and then we practiced a few times. Not only did turning and talking provide a social release, but it also helped students create better plans for their writing. Armed with more words and ideas from these brief conversations, they could more easily sit down and focus on writing.

➤ I also realized that I needed to rethink the materials used for writing and how students should access them during the transition. So I began using one-inch notebooks that were easier for students to manage. Then I did a quick Interactive Modeling lesson on how to efficiently get the notebook, a sharpened pencil, and paper.

➤ In addition, I had never adequately taught children what it looked like to get started writing. So I did an Interactive Modeling lesson on the exact path to take to one's seat and how to get right to work.

Once I took care of these issues, the differences were striking. Students wrote more and with higher quality. Because they now had the skills they needed, the transition to independent writing time became faster, more peaceful, and more efficient. This led to huge improvements in how students felt about writing—and it enabled them to focus more time and energy on the writing itself, leading to significant improvements in this essential academic skill.

In this chapter, you'll learn how to use Interactive Modeling to improve transitions. I hope that you'll see the same dramatic changes in students that I did.

——— Why Transitions Are ——— Challenging

✳

It's tempting to wonder why children can't just move from point A to point B. *How hard can it be?* But the simple truth is that people of all ages struggle with transitions. Pause for a moment right now and reflect on leaving your home for work. Do you worry whether your child has everything he or she needs for school? If your pet has water and food? What you need to pick up at the store after work? Transitions are hard. And for children, they are even harder!

There are many reasons why transitions are so challenging. For instance:

➤ If we're truly engaged in a task, it's very difficult to stop and change to another task. If this second task isn't as engaging, the transition is even harder. Think of children returning from recess or lunch to academics!

➤ We often have a lot of "stuff" to manage during transitions—both from the first task (cleaning up, filing something away, returning things to their proper place) and for the next one (finding what we need, getting it out, organizing it).

➤ Transitions frequently involve other people, many of whom may consider these intervals a good time for a little socializing (or a lot).

➤ Space (and how the space is organized) can add to the burden of transitions.

➤ Time constraints often mean we need to move quickly and efficiently, when many of us prefer a more leisurely pace.

Fortunately, Interactive Modeling can help address all of these challenges and make transitions go more smoothly. And smoother, happier transitions will help students feel safer, have more time to learn, and stay focused on the engaging work of school.

—— Transitions and ——
Interactive Modeling

✳

Arrival Times

The procedures you establish for what students do upon first entering the classroom set the tone for a positive, successful day—or for a frenetic, problematic one. If you reflect on your expectations for this time of day and plan how to use Interactive Modeling to help children reach these goals, you'll better ensure a successful start to the day.

What do you need to model with your students so they can get off to a great start? For example, younger students may need help with:

- Putting away coats and unpacking

- Greeting the teacher and other students

- Waiting patiently if other students are greeting the teacher

- Reading and interacting with the morning message that you wrote to the class

- Going quietly to sit down and getting to work

- Using an alternate attendance procedure (if you don't do roll call)

- Handing in homework, notes from home, and so on

- Knowing what to do if they come in late

- Doing other morning choices (for example, choosing a book from the classroom library to read or playing a math game with a partner)

For older students, rather than separately modeling how to do these tasks, you might want to combine several skills into one lesson (such as how to read the morning message, go quietly to a seat, and get to work writing in their journals). If students generally arrive all at once, you might use a shorter routine with fewer elements to model and focus more on student-to-student interactions.

The example on the next page shows how Ms. Yazdian, a second grade teacher whose students had a twenty-minute window for arrival, taught the basics of what to do during this time.

Arrival Time

1 Say what you will model and why:

Ms. Yazdian: "I'm going to show you what to do when you enter the class-room so that we all can have a safe, pleasant start to our day. Ryan, pretend to be the teacher. Martin and Kiana, pretend to be reading at your desks. I'm going to step into the hallway and then come back into the classroom. Watch and see what I do to take care of myself and others when I arrive."

2 Model the behavior:

Ms. Yazdian leaves the classroom and quickly reenters, stopping just inside the door. She smiles at Ryan (the teacher) and says, "Good morning, Ms. Yazdian." Then she walks directly to "her" desk, waving silently to Martin and Kiana, and begins to read a book.

3 Ask students what they noticed:

Ms. Yazdian: "What did you notice about how I took care of myself and others?"

Ava: "You said 'good morning' to the teacher."

Ms. Yazdian: "Why is it important to greet the teacher when you arrive?"

Diego: "You're being polite."

Ms. Yazdian: [*following up*] "Yes. Are there any other reasons?"

Valerie: "So the teacher knows you're there."

Ms. Yazdian: [*prompting more observations*] "What did I do after I greeted the teacher?"

Luis: "You went to your desk."

Jen: "You read a book at your desk."

Ms. Yazdian: [*following up*] "How did I get to my desk?"

Ava: "You walked."

Ms. Yazdian: [*prompting*] "How did I wave to Martin and Kiana?"

Diego: "Quietly."

Valerie: "You were friendly."

4 Invite one or more students to model:

Ms. Yazdian: "Who can show us how to come into the classroom and start the day the same way I did?" Ms. Yazdian chooses Anjali to demonstrate; she does all the steps just as Ms. Yazdian modeled.

5 Again, ask students what they noticed:

Ms. Yazdian: "What did you notice about the way Anjali entered the classroom and went to her seat?" Students point out the key behaviors; Ms. Yazdian calls special attention to how calm and friendly Anjali was.

6 Have all students practice:

Because having everyone wait for a turn to practice one after another would take too long, Ms. Yazdian has the class work on an engaging back-to-school assignment while she calls up a few students at a time to practice.

7 Provide feedback:

As students practice, Ms. Yazdian reinforces their positive behaviors privately.

Ms. Yazdian: [*reinforcing one student's initial successes*] "That's exactly how it should look and sound. You walked straight to your desk, waved silently to some friends, and got right to work."

One student gets a bit silly during the practice. She has him practice again.

Ms. Yazdian: [*privately*] "Show me how to enter the room calmly the same way I did."

After everyone has had a chance to practice and complete the assignment, Ms. Yazdian reinforces the successes of the entire class.

Ms. Yazdian: "Now you know how to start the day in our classroom. You know how to greet me, how to walk to your desk, how to wave silently to classmates, and how to read or work on an assignment at your desk. It looks like we're ready for a safe and productive start to our day tomorrow."

• •

To adapt this lesson for younger children:
Begin by modeling how to come in and say "hello" to
the teacher. Later, model where students should go
and what they should do there.

• •

To adapt this lesson for older children:
Expand the lesson to include handing in homework
and doing other morning tasks.

Transitions to Independent Work

The transition from instruction to independent work is especially challenging for children. They often have to move within a crowded space while carrying or collecting the required supplies. They must also retain the directions for the independent work assignment as they make this tricky transition.

Although many transition skills can be taught early in the year, transitions often become much more complex as the year progresses. In particular, assignments that require many kinds of materials, or multiple work partners, will also likely require additional Interactive Modeling lessons to teach how these elements should go together.

What do you need to model with your students to ensure smooth transitions to independent work? For example:

➤ Moving from circle/instructional area to seats, including traffic paths and noise level

➤ Getting materials (how, where, when)

➤ Finding a place to work with a partner or group

➤ Getting started on the assignment

➤ Knowing what to do if they forget directions or need something

➤ Handing out materials (for students who are helpers; see page 79)

To see how Mr. Lee, a fourth grade teacher, uses Interactive Modeling to teach a complicated transition from his mini-lesson to having partners play a game, take a look at the Interactive Modeling in Action example that follows.

15 minutes

Transition From Group Instruction to Working With a Partner

1 Say what you will model and why:

After teaching students a fraction game, Mr. Lee knows that they also need to learn how to efficiently find partners, get materials, and start playing the game.

Mr. Lee: "Our classroom rules say that we should do our best learning and take care of ourselves and our supplies. Pretend that Shawna is the teacher and Victor is my partner. Watch how Victor and I get started quickly, so we can spend more time playing the game and learning."

2 Model the behavior:

Mr. Lee has Shawna announce that Victor and Mr. Lee are partners. Mr. Lee audibly whispers to Victor, "You get the cards and two recording sheets. I'll get pencils and clipboards. Then, meet back here." After completing these tasks, Mr. Lee audibly whispers to Victor, "Where can we work?" Victor replies, "No one is in that corner. Let's go there." The two walk quietly to the corner, sit facing each other, place the cards between them, and get clipboards and pencils ready. Mr. Lee says, "Your first name comes first in the alphabet, so you're first." The two start playing the game.

3 Ask students what they noticed:

Mr. Lee: "What did Victor and I do to get quickly started on the game?"

Jack: "You divided up the jobs."

Mr. Lee: [*following up*] "How did we divide up those jobs?"

Bella: "Victor got the cards and recording sheets; you got the pencils and clipboards."

Mr. Lee: "What did we do next?"

Sydney: "You met back together and decided to work in an empty corner."

Mr. Lee: "Then what did we do?"

Jorge: "You walked calmly, sat down, and started playing."

Mr. Lee: [*following up*] "How did we sit?"

Amy: "Facing each other, with the cards in the middle."

Mr. Lee: "How did we decide who went first?"

Jack: "Quickly."

Bella: "You went by alphabetical order of your first names."

Mr. Lee: [*wrapping up*] "How long did it take Victor and me to get started? Show me with your fingers." [*most students hold up two fingers*] "Yes. This should take only two minutes."

4 Invite one or more students to model:

Mr. Lee: [*looking at his list of partners*] "Sonia and John, show us how to get started just like Victor and I did. Dani, time them. Everyone else, watch and see what they do."

5 Again, ask students what they noticed:

The class points out what Sonia and John did (as in Step 3); Dani notes that this transition took "exactly" one minute and forty-seven seconds.

6 Have all students practice:

Mr. Lee: "Find your partner on the list I posted. Then get started as quickly and carefully as Sonia and John did."

7 **Provide feedback:**

Two students immediately come over to ask Mr. Lee a question. Mr. Lee needs to observe the class, so he holds up his hand and tells them he'll check in with them after everyone is playing.

> Mr. Lee: [*reinforcing initial successes*] "I see partners dividing up the jobs and getting what they need. I see some people setting up their playing spot."

> Mr. Lee: [*to a pair taking too long to gather materials*] "Get what you need now. You need to start playing in one minute." He stands nearby to make sure they follow through.

When the other students are engaged in the game, he gives his attention to the students with the question. Then Mr. Lee reinforces the class's successes with this transition.

• •

To adapt this lesson for younger children:
Make baggies of all supplies they'll need for a game and model only finding a good place to work with one's partner.

• •

To adapt this lesson for older children:
Combine the teaching of the game rules, the recording of results, and the transition of getting started into one Interactive Modeling lesson. If students are generally skilled in transitions, you could do an abbreviated Interactive Modeling lesson that focuses just on the transition (see Chapter 7, pages 153–165, to learn more about abbreviated Interactive Modeling).

Transitions to Group Instruction

Students often struggle with the transition *from* an activity or assignment *to* group instruction. That's because, if we've done our jobs well, children will be fully engrossed in what they're doing and naturally have a hard time stopping and shifting gears.

What do you need to model with your students so they can efficiently move from working to sitting in the circle (or wherever you will be instructing) and being ready to listen? For example:

➤ Responding to the signal for quiet attention

➤ Listening to cleanup directions

➤ Cleaning up and organizing materials

➤ Putting away finished/unfinished work (where, how, when)

➤ Pushing in chairs

➤ Moving to the group instruction area with appropriate noise levels and finding a place to sit

For more on the care and cleanup of materials, see Chapter 4, beginning on page 83. See a sample Interactive Modeling script on transitioning from independent work to group instruction on page 190 in Appendix B.

Walking in Hallways

No matter what their ages, students need to learn to leave the classroom calmly and walk safely in the hallways. If they're too loud, they bother other classrooms. If they're not watching the person in front of them, they can get separated or even lost. If they touch artwork on the wall, it can get damaged . . . the potential for trouble can seem endless.

For these transitions to work effectively, collaborating with colleagues helps. If everyone can agree on hallway expectations, then every teacher can model and reinforce the same rules and behaviors. Transitions that involve spaces outside the classroom become much smoother when they're based on one set of schoolwide expectations. If your school does not have common expectations for hallway behavior, still model your expectations and explain the reasons for them, especially for younger children. Talk with your colleagues about creating common expectations and supporting one another in holding students to the same standards of behavior.

What do you need to model with your students so they can navigate the hallway with consideration and respect for one another and everyone else in school? For example:

➛ Lining up in the classroom (single line or pairs?)

➛ Walking pace and voice volume

➛ Carrying library books, backpacks, and other materials

➛ Doing a silent wave to say "hi" if they see someone they know

➛ Knowing what to do if they get separated from the class

➛ Keeping hands off displays and walls

➛ Knowing what to do if they pass a water fountain and are thirsty

➛ Acting as the line leader or the caboose (last in line)

For a sample Interactive Modeling lesson on walking in the hallways, see page 177 in Appendix B.

Entering Special Area Classrooms and Assembly Spaces

When students enter a new space, whether for an assembly or a special area class, we want them to do so calmly and quickly so they can focus their attention on learning. Again, schoolwide collaboration can be beneficial in planning these transitions.

If all teachers, including special area teachers, agree on basic entrance procedures, students will be much more likely to develop successful habits for them. Perhaps the schoolwide expectation is that students will stop at the special area classroom door and then, upon a teacher's signal, enter, sit at an assigned spot, and immediately engage in the task that's posted there. If, instead, each teacher has a set of unique expectations, then students have to remember to follow a different set of procedures for each special area classroom. They can do it, but do we really want to use their energy this way?

What do you need to model with students so they can enter special area classrooms and assembly spaces efficiently? For example:

- → Stopping at the entrance

- → Putting away backpacks, lunchboxes, and other items

- → Upon a signal, going straight to a designated area using an appropriate walking pace and noise level

- → Sitting at the designated area, following any directions for what to do, and responding to the signal for quiet attention

On the next page, you can see an example of how Mrs. Bautista, a music teacher, and Mr. Johnson, a classroom teacher, collaborated to teach sixth graders how to enter the music room ready to learn.

15 minutes

Entering the Music Room
Ready to Learn

1 Say what you will model and why:

Mr. Johnson, the sixth grade teacher, and Mrs. Bautista, the music teacher, gather the students together just outside the music room.

Mrs. Bautista: "We know that music is an important part of your education and many people's favorite class. We want to make sure you make the most of music time. So, we're going to show you how to enter the music room quickly and safely, get what you need, and be ready to start on time. Mr. Johnson and I are going to show you what that looks and sounds like. Watch and see what you notice us do. Go ahead and sit down on the risers."

2 Model the behavior:

Once the children are seated, the two teachers enter the room and walk directly to the instrument shelf. They pick up instruments in turn and go to where the music folders are. Then each takes a folder and sits in front of a music stand. Next each puts the instrument on the floor and the folder on the stand. They start reading a message Mrs. Bautista has posted that has clues about a composer. After reading, they quietly chat about which composer it might be.

3 Ask students what they noticed:

Mrs. Bautista: "What did you notice about how we entered the music room?"

Katie: "You were quiet."

Miranda: "You went to the instrument shelf and got your instrument. Then Mr. Johnson got his."

Mrs. Bautista: [*following up*] "Then what did we do?

Edward: "You went and got folders."

Anya: "Then you went to find a chair."

Mr. Johnson: "What did we do with our folder and instrument once we got to our seats?"

Dante: "You put your instrument on the floor and then you put the folder on the music stand."

Mr. Johnson: [*following up*]: "How long did all that take?"

Katie: "Maybe a minute?"

Mr. Johnson: [*following up*]: "How did we do it so quickly?"

Miranda: "You just went straight from one thing to another."

Mr. Johnson: "That will give you more time for music. So what was the last thing we did?"

Edward: "You read the message and talked about who the mystery composer is. By the way, I think I know who it is."

Mr. Johnson: [*following up*]: "Hold on to that thought! How did we talk about the secret composer so that we took care of ourselves and others?"

Anya: "You were pretty quiet."

4 Invite one or more students to model:

Mrs. Bautista: "We need three volunteers to show us how to enter the music room and get started in the same way we did."

5 Again, ask students what they noticed:

Mrs. Bautista: "What did you notice that Naphthali, Nora, and Jose did?" The class points out what they observed (as in Step 3).

6 Have all students practice:

Mr. Johnson: "Now we're all going to practice. Pretend it's the beginning of music class. Go back into the hall. Then enter the room, get what you need, and get started the same way we showed you."

7 Provide feedback:

The two teachers observe as the students enter the room, gather instruments and folders, and go to their seats. After students have chatted about the mystery composer, Mrs. Bautista raises her hand (the signal for quiet attention) so she can reinforce their success with this transition.

Mrs. Bautista: "You all came in quickly and safely. Everyone walked toward the instrument shelf, waited patiently, and got instruments quickly. You then got folders and went straight to your seats. You read the message and chatted about the mystery composer quietly. Doing that every time will give us plenty of time for our music lessons. Now, who thinks they know the mystery composer is?"

• •

To adapt this lesson for younger children:

Simplify it. For example, begin by modeling only going straight to seats, reading the message, and chatting with the person next to you. If you teach third or fourth graders, you might also include the skill of picking up a music folder on the way to one's seat.

For an Interactive Modeling script on entering the art room ready to learn, see Appendix B, page 187.

Dismissal Times

At the end of the day, both children and teachers are tired. Without planning and practice, dismissal time can feel harried. And an unpleasant dismissal experience can negatively color an otherwise positive and productive day of learning.

Since the end of the day isn't an ideal time for new learning, it's best to avoid teaching dismissal routines then if you can. Instead, devote some time earlier in the day to teach and practice what dismissal should look, sound, and feel like.

What do you need to model with students to help them successfully end their school day and leave school feeling positive about their learning? For example:

- Getting backpacks

- Packing up backpacks

- Completing end-of-day tasks (such as putting chairs on top of tables)

- Putting on coat and other outerwear

- Walking to a designated spot, such as a closing circle or dismissal line

- Saying good-bye to the teacher or another adult

- Waiting for their name to be called in a car line or other specific dismissal routine

For an Interactive Modeling script on dismissal routines, see Appendix B, page 178.

Other Transitions

Depending upon your school's schedule and setup, some or all students might have to make other transitions during the day. Interactive Modeling can also help these transitions go smoothly so that students have more time for learning. For example:

➤ *Quiet time*—To ease the transition from recess/lunch back into the classroom, some teachers give children a ten- or fifteen-minute quiet time. Model how to enter, get supplies, and settle in.

➤ *Transition to recess/lunch*—Children sometimes need to get coats, jackets, and lunch boxes as they make the transition from the classroom to recess/lunch. Model how to do this transition efficiently, dividing the modeling into bite-sized lessons.

➤ *Transition to and from special education classes*—If you have students who need to go to and return from these classes, model how each transition should look and sound.

—— Tips for Success With —— Transitions

✳

Plan the transition carefully.

Think through exactly how you want each transition to look, sound, and feel. Consider the key aspects of the transition and how Interactive Modeling will help you teach each part. Some questions to keep in mind:

➤ What are the goals for this transition? How do you want the transition to look and sound?

➤ What are the potential stumbling blocks (materials, space constraints, etc.)?

➤ Do you need to keep any developmental considerations in mind? For example, will children's motor abilities limit the supplies they can carry?

➤ What exactly do you need to teach children? Why do students need to do the transition in this specific way?

Collaborate with colleagues.

It's easy to get stuck doing things the same way we've always done them. Having a colleague observe a transition with fresh eyes can be an easy way to find the stumbling blocks. Even if you can't find time for this level of collaboration, talk with colleagues about how they have set up various transitions and dealt with the challenges those transitions presented.

Give children a sense of time and pacing expectations.

One of the biggest teacher-student disconnects for transitions is our different senses of time. Children may honestly think they are being quick while we wonder why they can't speed things up. Think through how long a transition will realistically take children. You don't want to devote too much time to transitions, of course, but it's equally important not to expect children to transition so quickly that they feel pressured or stressed. Once you set a realistic pace, call students' attention to it during your Interactive Modeling lessons. Also try to give students a concrete sense of timing. Some teachers sing a favorite song with students for a set number of rounds—by the end of the last round, students are more likely to be ready for their next task or activity. Other teachers play music or use a timer. Whatever option you choose, don't assume that children will naturally know how long a transition should take.

Use visual reminders.

Some transitions are so challenging that it's helpful to provide students with concrete, visual reminders of what's expected. For instance, for the writing transition discussed earlier in this chapter, I wish I had used an anchor chart like this one from the start.

Getting Started on Writing

- ✓ Get your writing notebook.
- ✓ Go straight to your table.
- ✓ Briefly greet your tablemates.
- ✓ Open your notebook to the starting point.
- ✓ Take a sharpened pencil.
- ✓ Start writing!

Keep children engaged.

We need to share with students why smooth transitions matter and keep students as engaged as possible during these times. When doing an Interactive Modeling lesson about walking from our classroom to lunch, I might introduce it by saying, "I want to make sure we have as much time for lunch as possible and that everyone arrives at the cafeteria as happy and as safe as when we left our classroom. Watch and see how I walk to make sure that happens." For longer transitions like this, it's also helpful to give students something to see or do on their way to another area. For example: "See how many squares you see on our way to the cafeteria. Then tell me at the cafeteria door."

Teach how to use waiting times productively.

Everyone's life involves waiting for something or someone. For every transition, think about how much waiting is involved. If students have more than a few seconds of waiting time, give them ideas for what to do, such as talking quietly, reading a book, or playing a quiet hand game. For an activity in which all students must wait to begin until everyone has what they need, such as a science experiment, teach students what that waiting should look and sound like—and why it matters. For younger children, a concrete waiting symbol, such as a sign that says "hands off for now," can be helpful.

Address space issues.

Often, transitions are challenging for students because of the way our classrooms are arranged. Check your room to see if you can remove or at least improve upon any space constraints. For instance, take a look at the traffic paths in your room to see if you can create a better flow to and from desks. If some obstacles are unavoidable, address them directly in your Interactive Modeling. In one school where I worked, children had to go down three flights of stairs to get to their physical education class. So, during the lesson, I explicitly pointed out the challenges of this space: "What did you see me do to keep myself and others safe as I walked down these stairs?"

Know your role.

Sometimes (well, many times!), I wished I could use a transition time to gather materials I needed. Or do a quick prep for another lesson. Or check my email. Or sip some needed caffeinated beverage. But the reality I accepted as best for me and my students was this: Transitions are a teaching time. Although students might eventually be able to do transitions independently, for the most part, they need us to watch and coach them from the sidelines. Our job is to let students know what they are doing well and to quickly help anyone who's off track get back on track.

Consider having student helpers.

Think about how transitions could be speeded up or made more efficient if one or more student helpers passed out paper or other needed supplies. Some teachers assign one child to be the "materials helper" for the whole class; others have one "materials manager" per table. For either option, remember to teach and give student helpers time to practice how to do this job most effectively.

Be consistent.

Once you've taken the time to teach transitions, stick to what you've taught. Nothing is more confusing to children than when we go against what we said! If you teach an entrance routine in which students are to come into the classroom, sit in the circle, and begin thinking about a posted question, stick to that procedure. If you need to deviate one day, be sure to explain why and how this should occur.

Remember to reinforce success.

For example, when students are walking in a line, watch how they're doing. Reinforce positive behaviors along the way. Remember to be specific and describe exactly what they are doing well: "You are all walking safely with your eyes forward and hands to yourself. I could barely hear you, so I know we let all the classes that we passed keep learning. It only took us two minutes to get from our classroom to the cafeteria. We beat our record!"

—— A Closing Thought ——

If students lose just two or three minutes for every transition at school, that can add up to a loss of thirty minutes of instructional time each day—that's two and a half hours lost *every week!* By spending just a little more time to plan, teach, and practice transitions, you will give students a wonderful gift—more time to learn and grow.

Points to Remember

✳

➤ *List the transitions that your students need to do efficiently.*

➤ *Reflect on what makes these transitions challenging for students.*

➤ *Know why the transition is important.* Connect transitions to classroom rules and learning goals.

➤ *Evaluate each transition.* Break it down into small steps. Depending upon students' needs and abilities, teach steps separately, in chunks, or all at once.

➤ *Plan Interactive Modeling lessons for each transition.* Think about the best time to teach each one. Spread out this teaching as needed.

➤ *Be consistent.* Once you teach a transition, stick with it. If needed, adjust as the year goes on and reteach.

➤ *Reinforce success.* Watch for big *and* small successes. Use positive teacher language to reinforce these and provide specific feedback.

• • • • • • • • • •

For more help using Interactive Modeling with transitions, use the Planning Guide and Timelines in Appendix A, pages 169–173.

Supplies and Interactive Modeling

Tips for Success With Supplies
99

Points to Remember
103

Supplies

Whenever I'm in a master teacher's classroom, I'm amazed at how old but well cared for many of the supplies are. My friend Gail Ackerman teaches students to use and care for oil pastels so well that each set lasts about ten years. She chooses high-quality oil pastels and her students use them year after year, creating beautiful, bright pictures. Other colleagues I know have intricate picture books that work perfectly even though hundreds of students over the years have pulled the tabs, lifted the flaps, and flipped through the pages.

When we take the time to teach children to care for and use classroom materials properly, the materials last. Students benefit in many other ways as well. Valuing school supplies gives students the message that the work of school is worthwhile. When students know that the tools of their trade are special and valued, they take greater pride in their work and learn more as a result. More globally, teaching children the skills of valuing and caring for what they have will serve them (and the planet) well after they leave school.

In this chapter, you'll learn some general guidelines for using Interactive Modeling to teach children how to use and care for classroom materials, whether those supplies are "high quality" or "good enough," new or old. Because it's impossible to cover every kind of material in this book, I've compiled a list of common materials for each content area and considerations for using Interactive Modeling to teach about those. You may also want to take an inventory of your own classroom supplies and create a similar set of lists. And, as in previous chapters, I give you some sample Interactive Modeling lessons that you can use or adapt. I hope you and your students will come to find the tools of school more useful and meaningful as a result of reading this chapter.

—— Supplies and —— Interactive Modeling

✳

Language Arts/Literacy

When you use Interactive Modeling to teach students how to effectively handle materials, they'll spend the majority of their language arts time actually reading and writing. Plan exactly which materials your students will need, and then use Interactive Modeling to teach exactly what students must know to use those materials safely and efficiently.

For an Interactive Modeling script on how to safely refill a stapler, see Appendix B, page 191.

Language Arts/Literacy		
Supply	**What to Model About Usage**	**What to Model About Cleanup/Storage**
Classroom library books	How to check out	How to reshelve
Clipboards	How to safely put papers on and off	Where/how to store
Hole punch	How to safely make holes in paper	Where/how to store
Listening center	How to play/rewind; how to adjust volume	Where/how to store headphones
Markers	Putting cap on end of marker while using; capping marker when done	Where/how to store
Paper	Where to start/end writing; which side of paper to use first	Where/how to recycle paper
Pencil and eraser	How to use pencil-top eraser; how to use eraser carefully so it doesn't rip paper	Where/how to store or place in pencil holder
Pencil sharpener	How to use it; what to do if someone else is using it	How to neatly empty shavings
Pop-up/ special books	How to push/pull tabs; how to gently lift flaps	How to reshelve
Stapler	How to safely staple; how to add staples (for older students)	Where/how to store
Three-ring binders/folders/ internal dividers	How to safely open and put papers in; how to use dividers and place papers in relation to dividers	Where/how to store

Math

It's tempting to assume that children, especially older children, already know how to use the basic tools of math (dice, playing cards, manipulatives). But resist that temptation! Many children do not have prior experience with these materials. Even if they do, they might never have been given clear expectations for their care and use. A brief Interactive Modeling lesson is often enough to ensure a math material's safe and appropriate use.

Math		
Supply	**What to Model About Usage**	**What to Model About Cleanup/Storage**
Calculator	How to remove cover; how to use keys to perform operations	How to put cover back on; where/how to store
Compass	How to safely insert pencil; how to draw circles, arcs, and so on	Where/how to carry and store
Dice	Where to roll; how to roll	Where/how to store
Math manipulatives	How to link cubes together, join sides of shapes, etc.	How to place in bin quietly; where to place bin on shelf
Playing cards	How to shuffle; how to hold in one's hand for a game	How to make sure all the cards are there; how to put a rubber band around them (or place in baggie)
Protractor	How to measure angles	Where/how to store
Ruler, meter stick	How to measure	How to place in storage
Spinner	How to use the spinner	Where/how to store
Tape measure	How to measure; how to pull out/retract	Where/how to store

For an Interactive Modeling script on how to clean up a set of math cards, see Appendix B, page 185; for a script on how to measure with a ruler, see Appendix B, page 184.

Science

Interactive Modeling is a perfect match for science, which, by its very nature, requires the careful, safe, and exact use of tools. Use your modeling lessons to make sure that students know exactly how a given tool should be used and why—for learning, exploring, and experimenting.

Science		
Supply	**What to Model About Usage**	**What to Model About Cleanup/Storage**
Aquarium, terrarium, animal cages	How to add water and feed animals	How to clean
Balance scale	How to place objects on scale; how to figure out which is heavier	Where/how to store; how to take apart, if appropriate
Eyedropper	How to get liquid into dropper; how to disperse liquid	How to clean; where/ how to store
Hand lens, magnifying glass	How to look at object through hand lens/magnifying glass	Where/how to store
Microscope	How to place slide under lens; how to adjust focus	Where/how to carry and store

Take a look at the Interactive Modeling in Action example that follows to see how Ms. Wood, a second grade teacher, taught the correct use of hand lenses and how to record one's observations. (Note that Ms. Wood uses a Think-Aloud strategy in her modeling. See Chapter 1, page 17, for more on using Think-Alouds.)

Using a Hand Lens and Recording Observations

1 Say what you will model and why:

Ms. Wood: "Today, we'll learn how to use a hand lens, just like scientists do to observe what they're studying. We'll also learn how to carefully record what we see. I want you to know what I'm thinking as I use the lens, so I'll have my 'Thought Bubble' up part of the time. Watch to learn what I'm thinking and doing."

2 Model the behavior:

Holding up the Thought Bubble, Ms. Wood says, "I'll start by just looking at the leaf and drawing its outline. I don't need the hand lens for that." She carefully puts down the hand lens and Thought Bubble, makes her drawing, and then peers at the leaf through her hand lens. Holding up the Thought Bubble again, she says, "I see lots of beautiful lines on this leaf. I'll draw the biggest ones first." After doing so, she then looks at and records the leaf's colors.

3 Ask students what they noticed:

Ms. Wood: "What did you notice about how I used the lens and recorded my observations?"

Kaleb: "You were careful."

Ms. Wood: [*following up*] "Why does that matter?"

Malia: "Well, scientists have to make sure they record what they're seeing."

Ms. Wood: "What did you notice about how I did my first drawing?"

Paul: "You put down the lens and studied the outline of the leaf."

Bianca: "You kept checking the leaf to make sure you were right."

Andre: "Could we trace the outline of the leaf?"

Ms. Wood: [*acknowledging second graders' need for such a support*] "Hmmm. Interesting idea. Sure, if that will help you; just remember that as scientists you want to be really careful how you handle your specimen." [*pauses*] "Now, what else did I do with the lens to make sure I could see all the details of the leaf?"

Kaleb: "You moved it back and forth a little."

Ms. Wood: "Yes, sometimes it can take a minute to get it in the right spot." [*following up*] "Why did I draw as I went along, rather than waiting until I was finished looking?" [*gives think time*]

Malia: "If you wait until the end, you might forget what you saw earlier."

Paul: "You might need to draw a little at a time to be careful."

4 Invite one or more students to model:

Ms. Wood chooses Serissa from among the eager volunteers and gives her the lens, a leaf, and an observation sheet.

Ms. Wood: "Serissa will show us how to use the hand lens to study another leaf and record her observations, just as I did. She won't be thinking aloud—just doing. See what you notice."

5 Again, ask students what they noticed:

Ms. Wood: "What did you notice about the way Serissa used the hand lens and recorded what she saw?" Students note that Serissa traced the leaf very carefully and counted its lines before carefully drawing them. She can see that children can't wait to start their own work.

6 Have all students practice:

Ms. Wood has her materials managers distribute supplies to each table.

Ms. Wood: "I have twenty-five different leaves. Take one leaf, and then use the hand lens and recording sheet the same way Serissa and I did."

7 Provide feedback:

Ms. Wood: [*to reinforce positive behaviors*] "I see everyone moving the hand lens carefully to get a good view and recording their observations as they go. I already see a lot of details recorded and careful drawing. Keep going!"

One student says he's already finished, but he's barely used the hand lens and drawn only a very basic leaf shape. Ms. Wood guides him to use the lens more and to record more exact observations. After a few minutes longer, she gathers the children around her.

Ms. Wood: [*to prompt student reflection*] "What do you think you did well as scientists today?" Students note that they observed and drew very carefully and that working quietly helped them do so. Ms. Wood then invites them to share something interesting about their leaf.

• •

To adapt this lesson for younger children:
Model just using the hand lens before adding the more complex skill of recording observations.

• •

To adapt this lesson for older children:
Before doing this lesson, talk with children about what they already know about using hand lenses (or whichever tool they'll be using) and use that information to tailor your lesson.

Technology

Many children today have a great deal of experience with technology. However, not *all* children will know how to use classroom technology or be able to figure it out on their own. Students also need to be taught the expectations for technology use at school, which may differ significantly from expectations at home. Interactive Modeling is a quick and effective way to teach children how to meet these school expectations.

Technology		
Resource	What to Model About Usage	What to Model About Cleanup/Storage
Desktop computer	How to start up and log on; how to respond to the signal for quiet attention when on the computer	How to sign out/log off/ shut down
Interactive whiteboard	How to move text around; how to use the stylus; how to use various programs	What to do if someone is ahead of you
Laptop computer, netbook, tablet	How to start up and log on; how to respond to the signal for quiet attention when using it; how to access various applications or switch screens; how to write with the stylus	How to sign out/log off/ shut down; how to put back on storage cart
Memory stick/ flash drive/ thumb drive	How to insert into USB port; how to save documents	How to safely remove from computer; where/ how to store
Printer/scanner	How to turn on; how to load paper; what to do if it jams; how to position item for scanning; how to retrieve scanned item	How to turn off; where paper is stored
Word pro-cessing and other software programs	How to enter text or data; how to highlight, delete, move, or copy text	How to close and save a document

For an Interactive Modeling script on storing a tablet computer on a cart, see Appendix B, page 193; for a script on how to cut and paste text on a computer, see Appendix B, page 189.

Art

Remember, the purpose of Interactive Modeling is to teach students any "nonnegotiable" uses for supplies. You can find many ways to teach students how to be creative, of course, but Interactive Modeling is for when you need students to do something in a specific way. For example, you may want students to be creative when they cut out shapes, but you want them to carry scissors just one way for safety's sake—and that's what you'd teach them with Interactive Modeling.

Art		
Supply	What to Model About Usage	What to Model About Cleanup/Storage
Calligraphy pens	How to make different thicknesses of letters; how to write in various styles	Where/how to store
Glue sticks	How far to roll up; how to apply	Rolling down, putting top on
Markers	Putting cap on end while using	Placing cap on tightly
Modeling clay	How to take out; how much to use	How to store so it won't dry out
Oil pastels	How to hold/use	How to place back in box; how to clean off desk
Paintbrushes, watercolors	How to hold; how to fill up water cup; how to get brush wet and dip into paint	How to wash and store; how to dispose of water
Portfolios	How to organize	Where/how to store
Scissors	How to hold and cut safely	How to carry/return to basket

Supply	What to Model About Usage	What to Model About Cleanup/Storage
Stamps, stamp pads	How to press stamp into pad; where/how to stamp on paper	How to clean stamp (or desk); where/how to store
Stencils	How to hold in place and use	Where/how to store
Tape	How much to use	Where/how to store
Wire	How to bend and shape; how to safely cut what you need	Disposing safely of scraps; where/how to store

For an Interactive Modeling script on how to use and store glue sticks, see Appendix B, page 179.

Music

Whether you're a classroom teacher who enjoys doing music with students or a music teacher, you can use Interactive Modeling to teach students specific ways to use and care for musical instruments. Not only will instruments and equipment last longer, but you and your students will have more time to actually enjoy the music.

Music		
Equipment	What to Model About Usage	What to Model About Cleanup/Storage
CD/audio player	How to turn on, how to insert CD; how to play/pause/stop; how to search for a selection	How to turn off; how to remove a CD and close player
Musical instruments	How to take out (and assemble, if needed); how to hold; how to play a specific note	How to put into cases or storage areas; what to do if someone is ahead of you
Papers, pencils, other supplies	Where/how to access; how to use during class	Where to store at end of class
Scarves, flags, other props	How to use safely and appropriately	Where/how to put away

PE/Recess

Although children are frequently told in a reactive way what they can and cannot do with playground equipment ("Eric, don't go up the slide—go down!"), a more effective approach is to proactively teach these expectations. Students will greatly benefit from the careful and deliberate teaching of the rules and skills for using any piece of equipment. To the extent you can, do some of this teaching indoors, where students can bring more attention to the lesson.

PE/Recess		
Resource	**What to Model About Usage**	**What to Model About Cleanup/Storage**
Cones	How to mark out an area	How to stack and store
Jump rope	How to jump; how to twirl for two-person jumping	Where/how to store
Playground equipment	How to slide down slide; how to swing; how to follow sandbox rules; how to wait for your turn	Where/how to store
Sports equipment	How to sign out equipment; how to throw/catch a ball or use a bat; how to wait for your turn; how to respond to the signal for quiet attention	How to sign in equipment; where/how to store

General Cleanup

No matter what materials are involved, you can use Interactive Modeling to teach general cleanup procedures. For example:

- ➤ Organizing one's desk, cubby, or locker

- ➤ Cleaning up big spills

- ➤ Wiping off tables

- ➤ Cleaning an area, including scanning to make sure nothing is left behind

- ➤ Using a broom, handheld vacuum cleaner, mop, or cleaning cloth

- ➤ Knowing what to do when they finish their cleanup duties

To see how Ms. Alvarez, a kindergarten teacher, used Interactive Modeling to help her students learn how to clean up the classroom after center time, take a look at the example that follows.

INTERACTIVE MODELING IN ACTION ✳ **K**indergarten

10 minutes

How to Clean Up an Area of the Classroom

1 Say what you will model and why:

Ms. Alvarez: "Our rules say that we will take care of each other and our classroom. When center time ends, those rules mean we have to carefully clean up. Let's pretend it's the end of center time and I've been playing in the block area. Watch to see how I clean up."

2 Model the behavior:

With the kindergartners gathered in the block area, which she's set up beforehand, Ms. Alvarez carefully puts the blocks away, checking the labels on the shelves to make sure each block goes back where it belongs. With most of the blocks put away, she scans the area and reacts visibly as she notices blocks that have "escaped" outside the block area. When she finishes cleaning up, she chooses a book from the bookshelf, sits down, and starts reading.

3 Ask students what they noticed:

Ms. Alvarez: "What did you notice about how I followed our rules as I cleaned up the block area?"

Maya: "You put them away."

Ms. Alvarez: [*following up*] "How did I do that?"

Gabriel: "You didn't throw them."

Ms. Alvarez: [*prompting for a positive statement*] "What *did* I do?"

Gabriel: "You put them on the shelf gently."

Ms. Alvarez: "How did I make sure that the blocks were in the right place?"

Arianna: "You looked at those pictures on the shelf."

Ms. Alvarez: [*reinforcing*] "Yes, these pictures and labels show which block goes in each place. And how much noise did I make while I was putting the blocks away?"

Carlos: "You were quiet."

Ms. Alvarez: "And how did I make sure I found all the blocks?"

Ella: "You stood up and looked around."

Ms. Alvarez: "How about when I finished cleaning—what did I do?"

Maya: "You got a book to read."

4 Invite one or more students to model:

Quickly setting out some more blocks, Ms. Alvarez asks for volunteers to model cleaning up. She chooses two children so that the class can see what a group cleanup looks like.

Ms. Alvarez: "Lexi and Tony are going to clean up the block area, just as I did. Watch and see what you notice."

5 Again, ask students what they noticed:

Ms. Alvarez: "What did you notice about the way Lexi and Tony cleaned up the block area?" Students note that the two children made sure the blocks were in the right places, checked for missing blocks, and so on (as in Step 3).

6 Have all students practice:

Because everyone can't practice cleaning up at once, Ms. Alvarez tells students that they'll have opportunities to practice throughout the week.

Ms. Alvarez: "During center time this week, I'll make sure that everyone gets a chance to practice cleaning up the block area. I'll watch and see how well we're doing with that. How will we know if we're taking good care of the blocks?"

Oscar: "They'll all be in the right place."

Arianna: "We won't find any under the shelf."

7 Provide feedback:

During the week, Ms. Alvarez makes sure different students clean up the blocks each day, guiding them as needed.

Ms. Alvarez: [*reinforcing positive behaviors*] "I see you using the labels on the shelves to help you decide where blocks go. I also see you placing them gently and quietly. I see you looking around to make sure you found all the blocks. That helps make sure they'll be ready for the next group."

• •

To adapt this lesson for older children:

Teach how to clean up several classroom areas in one Interactive Modeling lesson.

Tips for Success With Supplies

※

Plan thoughtfully.

Think carefully about Step 1, your opening statement. If students know why a material must be used in a particular way, they're more likely to do so. Also, plan your modeling for Step 2, so you show just what you expect them to do, nothing more or less. Then, pay close attention at Step 3, when students are noticing key aspects of your modeling. Remember to call their attention to any essential points they don't notice on their own.

Start with high-quality materials in good condition.

If materials are messy, damaged, hard to handle, or have missing parts, students will probably not take good care of them. Try to provide top-notch supplies that work the way they're supposed to and are well suited to students' developmental needs and abilities. If you have a limited budget, err on the side of having fewer but higher quality materials (for instance, with art supplies such as markers, watercolors, colored pencils, and glue sticks)—they'll last longer and lead to better student work. Use sites such as donorschoose.org or adoptaclassroom.org to help you purchase what you need. Also, ask a local charity or parent group for help. But remember, no matter what the quality of the supplies, children should know to value and care for them all.

To learn more about classroom setup and materials:

- *Classroom Spaces That Work* by Marlynn K. Clayton with Mary Beth Forton (Northeast Foundation for Children, Inc., 2001)

- *What Every Teacher Needs to Know,* K-5 Series by Mike Anderson and Margaret Berry Wilson (Northeast Foundation for Children, Inc., 2010–2011)

Visit www.responsiveclassroom.org for these and other resources.

Set up an easy-to-use organizational system.

Your organizational systems convey to students how much you value materials as learning tools. For instance, if you place supplies neatly in bins that are clearly labeled and house those bins on well-marked shelves, children will more likely follow your system. On the other hand, if storage areas are messy, if children don't readily understand the system used, or if they can't reach a bin without major effort, they're much more likely to lose, mis-place, or just shove things in mindlessly. Think about what is needed (and when) and organize accordingly. If you struggle with organization, find a colleague who is  gifted in this area and enlist his or her help. Organization matters: When you have it, your Interactive Modeling of materials is much more likely to produce effective and lasting results.

Think about what might go wrong.

One of the best lessons I learned during my pre-service work was to spend some time anticipating what might go wrong during any lesson. Specifically planning how to head off potential problems may seem like a doomsday way of thinking, but it's the key to being proactive, and it comes in especially handy when you teach how to use classroom materials properly. For each material students will be using, think through how they might misuse or misunderstand it. If, for example, children do not know how to use the $2,000 interactive whiteboard, they might write on it with a dry-erase marker. Plan your Interactive Modeling lessons to steer students clear of such unwanted outcomes.

Look at each material as a child would.

Sometimes we're so used to our adult way of seeing materials that we do not anticipate how a child might view them. I would never have thought of stretching tape off a roll as far as it could go, but it was the first thing one child tried when I introduced the class to tape. We do want to foster and encourage children's curiosity and expand their repertoire of how to use materials. But we also need to anticipate uses that might be dangerous or destructive and explicitly teach students how to use supplies safely.

Decide what you want to teach.

It's important to decide whether you want children to explore various creative uses of materials or to teach them one specific way to take care of those materials. If, for example, you want children to explore various paintbrush strokes and painting styles, you could use the *Responsive Classroom* strategy of Guided Discovery. (To learn more about Guided Discovery, visit www.responsiveclassroom.org.) But if you want to teach children a specific way to clean a paintbrush, you would use Interactive Modeling.

Make sure you practice in advance.

It's never a good idea to "wing it" with Interactive Modeling, but this is especially true with materials. We may be so familiar with some materials that we forget the complexities and challenges they may present for students. Take the time to plan and practice exactly what you will do when demonstrating. This way, you'll know exactly what you expect students to do and just what to highlight when you ask what they noticed about your modeling.

Remember to keep cleanup fun.

Cleaning up does not have to feel like drudgery. Indeed, it goes more smoothly when it feels like a fun time or a challenge. Let your class select their own cleanup songs and play them as part of cleanup routines. (See the next page for song ideas.) Or make cleaning up a game, challenging your students to clean up as quietly and as quickly as possible, or while using only deep voices, or standing on tiptoe, or in numerous other ways.

Cleanup Song Ideas

Teachers often ask me if I know the "perfect" cleanup song. The truth is there isn't one, but here are some things to consider in choosing great cleanup songs:

■ *What can you stand to listen to over and over again all year?* You want songs to become part of your cleanup routines, so they need to be ones that won't get stuck in your head and annoy you.

■ *How long do you want cleanup to last?* You'll need to choose the appropriate length song(s) for each cleanup routine.

■ *Does your class need a pick-me-up or a calming down cleanup song?* What else do you know about students, such as their musical tastes, that might be important to consider?

Here are a few cleanup songs to try:

Grades K–3 "A Spoonful of Sugar" from the movie *Mary Poppins*; "Don't Worry, Be Happy" by Bobby McFerrin

Grades 4–6 "Shower the People" by James Taylor; "Linus and Lucy" (the *Peanuts* theme song)

Reinforce success.

Be sure to let students know when you see them using, caring for, and storing materials carefully and thoughtfully. To students who store recess equipment appropriately, you might say, "I see that the balls are all safely back in the bin, the jump ropes are coiled and ready to use again, and the cones are neatly stacked. You did that all in five minutes." Letting students know that you see them taking good care of supplies reinforces the message that classroom materials matter and are essential to their learning.

——— A Closing Thought ———

Teaching children how to care for materials will help them truly value the "tools" of their classrooms—and that appreciation will carry over into their learning. And when they know how to care for things, you'll spend less time nagging them, cleaning up, and replacing supplies. It's another simple but powerful way that Interactive Modeling can make school life easier for all, provide more time for learning, and teach students lifelong skills and habits.

Points to Remember

✳

➤ *Think about what supplies students need to use now* and how you want students to use and care for those supplies.

➤ *Emphasize how using and caring for supplies connects to classroom rules and learning goals* when you plan and teach your Interactive Modeling lessons.

➤ *Model one way to do something*—Interactive Modeling works best when there is an expected way to use, care for, and store supplies.

➤ *Evaluate your expectations* and reevaluate as things change. Provide support to students who struggle with using supplies.

➤ *Reinforce success often*—focus on the positives you see and the progress students are making.

• • • • • • • • • • • • • •

For more help with using Interactive Modeling to teach students how to use and care for classroom supplies, use the Planning Guide and Timelines in Appendix A, pages 169–173.

Academic Skills and Interactive Modeling

Academic Skills

Interactive Modeling can help students master a wide variety of academic skills, such as using an index to locate information, following the steps of a mathematical algorithm, and discussing a science topic with a partner. Interactive Modeling can bring these skills to life in the classroom because students get to actively observe, describe, and practice each skill. As a result, children become more engaged in how they work and learn.

Without active engagement in learning these skills, it's easy for students to miss critical information. When my nephew was in first grade, my brother and sister-in-law asked me to do some individual work with him because he was struggling to learn to read. One day, we were working on some reading strategies and he said, "You know what, Aunt Margaret, I think my teacher has been talking about this same stuff."

It turns out that my nephew hadn't realized that what his teacher was saying at the front of the classroom applied to him and his reading. Once he made that connection, he began paying more attention at school. His parents, his teacher, and I also checked in on his understanding more regularly, and his reading and performance in other academic subjects quickly improved. Interactive Modeling can keep us from talking on and on *at* our students and instead draw them in, allowing them to make discoveries on their own, with active guidance from us.

When I taught kindergarten, I used Interactive Modeling to teach children a basic strategy for sounding out words. This lesson came after children had learned letter names and sounds and had developed an awareness of how sounds make up words. When they were ready, rather than just give a little lecture on sounding out words, I used Interactive Modeling. As I started, I asked students to be detectives and figure out what I was doing and why. After I demonstrated the skill and asked students what they noticed about how I had sounded out a word, I remember one of them saying, "You were like a detective, too! Each letter gave you a clue and you put them together to figure out the word."

From then on, the class saw sounding out words as an intriguing process—and when someone had trouble sounding out a word, a classmate would say, "Do you want help with the clues?" This lesson had much more impact than it would have if I had just told students what to do.

In this chapter, you'll explore how to plan Interactive Modeling lessons to teach general study skills and test-prep skills, as well as skills that are specific to certain academic and special area subjects. The Interactive Modeling structure helps students to carefully notice and specifically describe key aspects of these skills. It also enables them to see multiple successful examples of each skill in action. As a result, students are better able to internalize—and ultimately master—these critical learning skills.

Academic Skills and Interactive Modeling

✳

Study Skills and Test-Prep Skills

Many study skills and test-prep skills, such as turning and talking with a partner about a topic, highlighting important text, taking notes, and following directions, are essential to students' becoming successful life-long learners in all subject areas. We need to explicitly break down these processes and teach children how to use them so that every student becomes skilled at researching, analyzing, and evaluating information in class, during group work, and on their own. Interactive Modeling is a powerful and effective way to teach skills such as the following:

STUDY SKILLS AND TEST-PREP SKILLS

- Ask questions (as a listening skill and general reading skill)
- Head one's paper
- Fill out and check answer sheet
- Highlight important text
- Make/use a graphic organizer
- Take notes
- Make/play games or quiz oneself to study facts

- Partner chat
- Record observations and results
- Respond to questions in complete sentences
- Fill in answer selection
- Use test-answering strategies, such as process of elimination

The example that follows shows how Ms. Mishra, a fifth grade teacher, used Interactive Modeling to teach a way to answer textbook and test questions in complete sentences.

30 minutes

Responding to Questions in Complete Sentences

1 Say what you will model and why:

Ms. Mishra: "When you write your answers to homework assignments or tests, it's just like any other piece of writing. You need to think of your audience and communicate as clearly as possible so they can read what you've written and understand it immediately. I'm going to show you one way to make sure your answers are clear and easy to read. Watch and see what you notice."

2 Model the behavior:

On the electronic whiteboard, Ms. Mishra displays a question from a recently completed social studies lesson: "What were some of the reasons the Pilgrims came to the New World?" Beneath the question she writes, "Some of the reasons the Pilgrims came to the New World were religious freedom, economic opportunity, and adventure."

3 Ask students what they noticed:

Ms. Mishra: "What did you notice about how I made sure my answer was clear?"

Sophia: "You wrote a complete sentence."

David: "Your sentence made sense."

Ms. Mishra: [*following up*] "How did I use words from the question to help me with my answer?"

Camilla: "You used the part of the question that said 'some of the reasons the Pilgrims came to the New World' to start your answer."

Ms. Mishra: [*nodding*] "Doing that tells your audience exactly what you're writing about so that they don't have to reread the question. It also helps you to make sure that you write in complete sentences."

4 Invite one or more students to model:

Ms. Mishra chooses Antonio, whom she's fairly sure can apply the skill she's teaching, and posts the next question on the whiteboard.

Ms. Mishra: "Watch how Antonio uses that strategy to answer our next question."

5 Again, ask students what they noticed:

After Antonio writes his complete-sentence answer on the whiteboard, Ms. Mishra invites student observations.

Ms. Mishra: "What did you notice about the way Antonio answered the question?"

John: "He used words from the question in his answer."

Emmy: "He wrote a complete sentence."

Ms. Mishra: "Does his answer make sense?" [*students nod*] "Is it clear?" [*students call out, "Yes—really clear!"*]

6 Have all students practice:

Knowing that students struggle to consistently answer questions with complete sentences, Ms. Mishra wants to give them extra support, so she has them practice orally.

Ms. Mishra: "Now I'm going to pose two questions. With your partner, choose one question each and practice answering it the same way Antonio and I did."

7 Provide feedback:

Circulating and listening, Ms. Mishra quickly types up a few example responses she's heard and then calls the students' attention back to her.

Ms. Mishra: "I noticed that in all of these examples, you used a complete sentence that made sense. You started your sentences by using some of the words from the question. That helps ensure that your sentence answers the question."

Ms. Mishra adds another layer of practice by sending students off in pairs with some questions. Then she circulates again, coaching them along.

Ms. Mishra: [*reinforcing successes*] "I see that you used words from the question, and your answer is factually correct. You used a complete sentence, too." [*redirecting*] "I see that you started your answer with 'because.' Remember to use parts of the question to make sure your answer is complete. Let's try that together."

• •

To adapt this lesson for younger children:
Use a similar lesson structure to teach more basic skills,
such as figuring out the key words in a question and using
them in writing complete sentences for answers.

Language Arts/Literacy Skills

Learning to read, spell, and write involves a host of skills, many of which can be taught through Interactive Modeling. Even writing just one sentence requires children to know a specific set of skills—where to start and stop writing on the paper, how to indicate when one word ends and another begins, what kind of punctuation to use, and so forth.

Here's a short list of the kinds of detailed language arts and literacy skills you can teach with Interactive Modeling:

LANGUAGE ARTS/LITERACY SKILLS

- Add descriptive details to your writing
- Address an envelope
- Complete a story map or other graphic organizer for understanding a story
- Decide what's important vs. what's interesting in a text
- Diagram sentences
- Find a word in a dictionary or thesaurus
- Form plurals
- Give a book talk
- Give peer feedback on writing
- Read with a partner
- Reread what you wrote to make sure it makes sense
- Sort words according to phonetic or spelling patterns
- Summarize
- Use a table of contents or index
- Use a word wall or other reference to help spell a word
- Use appropriate punctuation
- Use editing marks
- Where to start/stop on the paper

To read a sample Interactive Modeling script on using the dictionary, see page 186 in Appendix B; for a sample script on giving a partner feedback, see page 194 in Appendix B.

Math Skills

Although much of elementary school math is exploratory, students are also expected to learn certain math techniques. For example, a third or fourth grade teacher may have students explore division by devising their own problem-solving strategies, but she may also teach students a specific process for long division. And it's with these specific processes that Interactive Modeling can be useful, helping you teach a range of math skills and techniques, such as the following:

MATH SKILLS

- Add up the value of a set of coins
- Read and interpret a graph
- Create a graph (using graph paper or a computer program)
- Record strategies or show work
- Sort objects
- Align numbers with decimal points in vertical form
- Use a formula (such as for calculating circumference)
- Use algorithms for basic operations, adding/subtracting fractions, and so on
- Use clues in a word problem to figure out which strategy to apply
- Round numbers up or down
- Convert fractions to percents and vice versa

To read a sample Interactive Modeling lesson on sorting and recording the results, see page 181 in Appendix B.

Science and Social Studies Skills

Both science and social studies require students to pay close attention to details. For students to become capable observers, researchers, data collectors, and experimenters, they have to learn certain techniques and processes. Interactive Modeling can help teach basic, yet essential, science and social studies skills, such as the following:

SCIENCE SKILLS	SOCIAL STUDIES SKILLS
➤ Conduct an experiment or parts of an experiment	➤ Conduct an interview to collect information
➤ Paraphrase a research source	➤ Paraphrase a research source
➤ Plant a seed, create a terrarium, etc.	➤ Preview a text using text and graphic features
➤ Preview a text using text and graphic features	➤ Put events in order on a timeline
➤ Record observations/ results of an experiment	➤ Use an atlas
	➤ Use the key/legend on a map to help read and interpret the map

For an example of how Ms. Evans, a third grade teacher, used Interactive Modeling to teach how to paraphrase key ideas from a research source, read the lesson that follows.

30–45 minutes

Paraphrasing a Research Source

1 Say what you will model and why:

Ms. Evans: "When authors write books, their words are protected by copyright laws. Those laws say that we can use facts we learn from these authors, but we can't just take what they've written word for word. We have to write in our own words. I'm going to show you what it looks like to record some facts you learn from a research source in your own words, not the author's words. I want you to follow my thoughts as I work, so I'll be thinking aloud some of the time."

2 Model the behavior:

On the electronic whiteboard, Ms. Evans displays and reads aloud a paragraph about the artist Frida Kahlo and then switches to a "note-card" screen with the word *Childhood* at the top. Showing her Think-Aloud sign, she records the key things she remembers from the paragraph.

Ms. Evans: "Let's see, she was born in Mexico in—I'd better check the year." [*She goes back to the first screen briefly and finds the date.*] "1907. OK, her parents had an unhappy marriage. She had two sisters. She was sick as a girl."

3 Ask students what they noticed:

Ms. Evans: "What did you notice about how I recorded what I read?"

Omar: "You wrote it your own way."

Ms. Evans: [*following up*] "What do you mean?"

Omar: "Your sentences don't sound like the ones you read out loud. You didn't copy them."

Ms. Evans: [*prompting for deeper thinking*] "What did I do to make sure that I didn't copy exactly what the book said?" [*seeing students' perplexed looks, she gives them think time*]

Gianna: [*tentatively*] "You didn't look at the paragraph?"

Ms. Evans: "That's right. Why might that matter?"

Edgar: "Well, unless you have a photographic memory, if you don't look, you can't copy."

Ms. Evans: "That's true. What else did I do to make sure I didn't copy?"

London: "Your sentences were much shorter. They just had the facts."

Ms. Evans: "Yes, I tried to write down just the key ideas—not everything. And what did I do when I couldn't remember something specific—like that birth date?"

Axel: "You went back to the paragraph, but you just looked quickly."

Ms. Evans: "Yes, I wanted to make sure I was accurate, but I tried to be fast so I wouldn't copy."

4 Invite one or more students to model:

Ms. Evans chooses Julian to model. She then displays the next paragraph and has the children read it silently. When Julian is ready, she switches to the "notecard" screen.

Ms. Evans: "Now watch while Julian records key ideas from the paragraph in his own words."

5 Again, ask students what they noticed:

After Julian writes a few notes, Ms. Evans invites student comments.

Ms. Evans: "What did you notice about how Julian recorded what he discovered?"

Ani: "He looked away from the paragraph while he was writing."

Jerome: "He wrote short sentences with just facts in them."

6 Have all students practice:

Ms. Evans wants all students to practice on the same text so that she can provide on-the-spot coaching.

Ms. Evans: "Now we're all going to practice. Read the next paragraph to yourself. Then, in your own words, tell your partner some of the facts you learned."

7 Provide feedback:

Ms. Evans circulates, listening carefully. She then calls the class together, records key facts from a few pairs, and displays the original text.

Ms. Evans: [*reinforcing successes*] "I noticed that lots of you chose only important facts, not all the details in the original text. I also noticed that you put those facts into your own words."

After another round of practice, she sends the students off to practice independently with their own source text. She has one small group of students who were struggling work closer to her so that she can continue to support their growth.

• •

To adapt this lesson for younger children:
Use a similar structure to teach a lesson on deciding between what is important and what is just interesting in a text.

• •

To adapt this lesson for older children:
Teach a similar lesson focused on more complex strategies for paraphrasing.

Special Area Skills

Just as is true for core subject skills, Interactive Modeling is a powerful tool for helping students learn specific skills in PE, music, art, and other special areas. In PE, for example, teachers may want to give students the freedom to explore many different types of balls, but they also expect students to learn how to throw each ball in an appropriate way.

SPECIAL AREA SKILLS			
PE	**Music**	**Art**	**Technology**
➤ Climb on an apparatus	➤ Count beats according to musical notation	➤ Create perspective in a drawing	➤ Comment on a blog or website
➤ Jump rope	➤ Keep the beat to a song	➤ Do special techniques like screen printing	➤ Compose/ send email
➤ Kick/hit a ball	➤ Play a musical instrument along with a recording	➤ Make a sketch	➤ Conduct an Internet search using a search engine
➤ Perform exercises (sit-ups, push-ups, etc.)		➤ Mix paints carefully	
➤ Run safely			
➤ Shoot/ dribble a basketball			
➤ Tag safely			
➤ Throw/ catch a ball			

The Interactive Modeling in Action box on the next page shows the way Ms. Moreau, an art teacher, taught kindergartners how to systematically experiment with mixing paint colors so they could remember what they discovered.

INTERACTIVE MODELING IN ACTION ✳ **K**indergarten

30–35 minutes

Mixing Paint

1 Say what you will model and why:

Ms. Moreau: "Today, we're going to experiment with mixing two or more colors of paint and seeing what color comes out. I want to make sure we all do this carefully so that we can all remember what we discovered. Then we'll talk about our discoveries. I'm going to mix a few colors of paint. Watch and see what you notice."

2 Model the behavior:

Ms. Moreau dips her paintbrush in the red paint on her pallet and makes a large red spot on the paper she's placed on an easel. She uses a paper towel to clean the brush off. Next, she dips her brush in yellow and paints a spot next to the red so that part of the yellow is mixed with the red and part remains separate, looking almost like a Venn diagram. She cleans her brush and turns back to the class.

3 Ask students what they noticed:

Ms. Moreau: "What did you notice me do when I mixed these two colors [*pointing to red and to yellow*]?"

Van: "You were careful."

Ms. Moreau: [*digging deeper*] "What did I do that was careful?"

Nyla: "You weren't all sloppy with the paint."

Ms. Moreau: [*prompting students to focus on details*] "How did I paint so that I'll be able to remember that red and yellow make orange?"

Dalila: "You left a little yellow and a little red on the sides, and you mixed them in the middle."

Ms. Moreau: [*following up*] "What did I do with my brush after each color?"

Dalila: "You wiped it off."

Ms. Moreau: "Why does that matter?" [*gives think time*]

Zaid: "Because you don't want to mix all the colors?"

Ms. Moreau: [*prompting*] "Why not?"

Zaid: "Well, if you had red on your brush and then you wanted to see what red and yellow made, it would be too messy."

4 Invite one or more students to model:

Ms. Moreau: "Now, watch how Liza mixes blue and yellow in the same way that I mixed red and yellow."

5 Again, ask students what they noticed:

Ms. Moreau: "What did you notice about how Liza mixed the colors?"

Shaila: "She did it like you did!"

Ms. Moreau: "Well, what did we both do?"

Anton: "She put one color on one side and one on the other."

Ms. Moreau: "What else did she do?"

Lina: "She remembered to wipe off the paintbrush."

Ms. Moreau: [*emphasizing a key point*] "When did she wipe off the brush?"

Baron: "She wiped it off every time."

Ms. Moreau: [*following up*] "What do you mean by 'every time'?"

Baron: "Every time she wanted a new color or to mix colors."

Mrs. Moreau asks one more volunteer to model a slightly harder task (combining Steps 4 and 5).

Ms. Moreau: "Terrance, this time, I want you to mix three colors—red, blue, and yellow. I'll help you if you need me to."

Terrance does well on his own, and his classmates are excited to see that he made purple. They notice that he mixed the paint only in the middle and wiped off his brush each time he painted.

6 **Have all students practice:**

Ms. Moreau: "Now we're all going to have a chance to practice. I'm going to give you each a pallet of paint and a brush. Try out a few different combinations of paint on your paper and see what you find out. At the end of art class, you'll have a chance to share your discoveries."

7 **Provide feedback:**

Ms. Moreau: [*reinforcing positive behaviors in private*] "Maddy, I see you're being careful to leave a little patch on both sides so you can remember what you did." "Dana, I notice you're being careful to get the old paint off the brush before you put new paint on." "Tomas, you kept your colors so clear that I can see that red and white make pink."

After cleanup, Ms. Moreau gathers the class and shares that she noticed almost everyone taking care to mix their colors and clean their brushes. The children excitedly respond to her invitation to share what they discovered about mixing paint colors.

• •

To adapt this lesson for older children:

Discuss what they already know about mixing paint colors and recording results, and use that to plan an abbreviated modeling lesson (see Chapter 7, starting on page 153).

To read a sample Interactive Modeling lesson on using rhythm sticks, see page 180 in Appendix B; for a script on throwing a ball overhand, see page 188 in Appendix B.

Special Education

Interactive Modeling can be highly effective with students who are receiving special education services, especially when you individually tailor lessons for students. For instance, some students might need processes broken down into smaller steps. If you were teaching the lesson on page 108 about writing answers to questions in complete sentences, you could highlight key parts of the question as you read it. Then you could highlight those same words when you use them in the answer.

Some students might also need more remodeling and support during the practice phase of Interactive Modeling. For example, if you used a lesson like the one on page 114 to teach paraphrasing, you might want to coach students through their first practice. Then you could remodel the skill in a small group or individual setting to support those students who are struggling.

Students also benefit when they receive frequent, specific feedback about their progress. You might want to break more complex skills into separate steps and check off (or let students check off) when they complete each step. For instance, after using Interactive Modeling to teach dictionary skills (see Appendix B, page 186), use a checklist like the one shown to point out to students that they've completed each step in the process.

Finally, some students might need separate individual or small group Interactive Modeling lessons on skills that their same-age peers have already mastered.

DICTIONARY SKILLS Checklist

- ✓ Find first letter of the word.
- ✓ Look for that letter section in the dictionary.
- ✓ Scan pages until you find words that have the same first letters as the word.
- ✓ Use the guide words at the top to find the exact page where the word is listed.
- ✓ Once you are on the right page, scan down until you find the word.

For example, in a fourth grade classroom, some students might need their teacher to model the steps for multidigit addition while their classmates might have moved on to multidigit multiplication.

TIPS FOR INTERACTIVE MODELING WITH STUDENTS RECEIVING SPECIAL EDUCATION SERVICES

- ➤ Break skills down as needed.
- ➤ Model separate or different skills as needed.

- ➤ Provide frequent, specific, positive feedback.
- ➤ Remodel and assist during practice phase as needed.

English Language Learners

For students whose primary language is not English, Interactive Modeling is a powerful strategy for teaching academics. That's because it builds in multiple demonstrations and gives students opportunities to describe for themselves the steps involved in the modeling. To heighten the effectiveness of Interactive Modeling lessons for English language learners, consider these steps:

➤ Use a "turn-and-talk" strategy before calling upon individual students to point out what they noticed in Steps 3 and 5. Allowing students to talk with a peer about what they noticed gives English language learners more time to practice speaking and listening in a more relaxed, private setting.

➤ For multistep processes, provide anchor charts or other visual reminders of the steps you modeled. Use pictures and photos to make these visual reminders even more powerful.

➤ Think about any key vocabulary that students might need to successfully understand a particular Interactive Modeling lesson. Preteach or review that vocabulary.

➤ Check in with students during the practice phase (Step 6) and reinforce their positive efforts. It's natural for some English language learners to be unsure about the key points of more complex Interactive Modeling lessons. Follow up to be sure students know exactly how to apply what you taught and to let them know when they are on the right track.

—— Tips for Success —— With Academic Skills

✳

Have a clear learning goal.

Defining exactly what you expect students to be able to do at the end of the lesson will help you more effectively plan your modeling (Step 2) and your questioning of students (Step 3). When you demonstrate what an academic skill should look and sound like, and call students' attention to its key components, students will be much more likely to retain and apply that skill. For instance, if you're going to use Interactive Modeling to teach children how to navigate an index in a book, think through what you want them to know and do with the index. For example: "Children will be able to locate several topics in the index, go to the referenced pages, and discover basic information about those topics."

Embed Think-Alouds in your modeling lessons as needed.

Especially when learning content area skills, children need to know what we're thinking as we model these skills. Plan for how to make your thinking visible in a brief, focused way, rather than as part of a lengthy explanation. For example, when teaching children the algorithm for double-digit addition, you may want to use a Think-Aloud as you regroup the tens. When you use the Think-Aloud strategy with younger students, make sure they understand that while you're talking out loud to demonstrate your thinking, you do not want them to talk when they practice the skill. See page 17 in Chapter 1 for more about using a Think-Aloud strategy.

Chunk complex processes into bite-sized pieces.

Some academic processes are complex enough that you may need to have students describe what you are doing throughout your modeling, rather than waiting until you have completed modeling the entire process. For instance, in teaching students how to record their observations for a science workshop, you may want to break down your modeling like this: model making one observation and recording it, followed immediately by students describing what they noticed; then make another observation and recording, and again ask students what they noticed, and so on. Dividing complicated processes into bite-sized pieces helps students stay engaged and develop deeper understandings.

Choose engaging tasks for practice sessions (Step 6).

Students are more likely to have lasting and positive memories of the academic skills they need if they practice those skills in ways that are meaningful and fun. If students are going to practice using a map key or legend, let them choose the map or area if possible. When they need to practice using editing marks, let them do so on a funny, intriguing, or especially relevant piece of text. Give as much time and thought to how and what students will practice in Step 6 as to the rest of your Interactive Modeling lesson.

Repeat Interactive Modeling lessons as needed.

Many academic skills take a great deal of time and practice to master, so students typically need to see these skills modeled multiple times. It's not a sign of failure if students need you to repeat your Interactive Modeling lessons. For instance, when teaching students how to perform certain math operations, it's unrealistic to think that a single modeling and practice session will be sufficient for mastery.

Plan to repeat your Interactive Modeling lesson as often as needed, such as when you notice students struggling or if some time has passed since they last used the skill. Also, vary the Interactive Modeling to keep students fully engaged each time. For instance, I varied my Interactive Modeling lessons on sounding out words by sometimes adding physical movements as I moved from letter to letter, using a Think-Aloud to illustrate letter combinations that were proving tricky, or using silly nonsense words during the modeling—something my students found very entertaining. Also, consider using an abbreviated Interactive Modeling lesson for reteaching skills (see Chapter 7, pages 153–165).

Ask yourself if Interactive Modeling is the best way to teach the skill.

Interactive Modeling is a powerful way to demonstrate various academic skills and have students notice key aspects, but it's not always the only or best way. Sometimes direct instruction is best. At other times, a more open, "constructivist" approach will be most effective for reaching students. For instance, when beginning to teach children double-digit addition, the math curriculum might call upon them to develop their own strategies for adding before being introduced to a formal method. Use your knowledge of the subject area, the curriculum, and students' needs and abilities to decide how best to teach a given skill.

Differentiate instruction with Interactive Modeling.

As you plan to use Interactive Modeling for academics, think about the various learning needs and levels of your students. You might decide to use Interactive Modeling to teach a skill to the whole class, but then you might differentiate the practice portion of the lesson (Step 6). For instance, you might use Interactive Modeling to teach the whole class how to find and use a thesaurus, but you might give different sets of practice words to students depending upon their reading or comprehension level. Or, you might ask one group of students merely to find synonyms and another group to find the correct synonym to use in a set of sentences.

You may also find yourself using Interactive Modeling in small groups to teach different skills to different students. For instance, when teaching math, you might use Interactive Modeling to teach one small group how to compare fractions while on the same day you use a different modeling lesson to teach another group how to add fractions.

Use technology wisely.

Although an interactive whiteboard or projector is a useful tool for Interactive Modeling of academic skills, it's not essential. You could also enlarge the page in question on the copier and display it, recreate key pieces of the text on chart paper, or let students use the textbook.

Reinforce success.

As students practice, point out exactly what they are doing well and how that can impact their academic performance. Doing so will help cement the learning from your initial Interactive Modeling lesson. For instance, to a student who has made and used a graphic organizer to brainstorm writing ideas, you might say, "I see you're using the technique we learned to think about your writing before you start. Having your ideas organized will help you make smart decisions as you write."

——— A Closing Thought ———

Because Interactive Modeling fully engages students in their learning, they're better able to master academic and study skills that are essential for their success both inside and outside of school.

Points to Remember

✳

➤ *Think about the specific academic skills or processes that students need to know how to do in one particular way.*

➤ *Break up complex skills into bite-sized pieces.*

➤ *Plan Interactive Modeling lessons with specific learning goals in mind.* Include "Think-Alouds" as needed.

➤ *Reteach Interactive Modeling lessons to the whole group, small groups, and individuals as needed.*

➤ *Address individual students' needs.* Evaluate students' progress and adjust lessons accordingly, providing extra support when appropriate.

➤ *Keep Interactive Modeling lessons engaging so that students stay engaged.*

➤ *Reinforce success often.* Focus on the positives you observe and the academic progress students are making.

• • • • • • • • • • •

For more help using Interactive Modeling with academic skills, use the Planning Guide and Timelines in Appendix A, pages 169–173.

Chapter 6

Social Skills and Interactive Modeling

Tips for Success With Social Skills

Points to Remember

Social Skills

Just about all adults stumble with certain social skills at one time or another. People interrupt conversations, "one-up" others when they're telling a story, have trouble accepting a compliment, or give insincere apologies. I wish that in the course of my own life, I had picked up the social skills of making pleasant small talk, walking up to a group of unfamiliar people and chatting at a party, and asserting myself by saying "no" when I'm overextended.

The simple truth is that social skills do not develop by osmosis when we're children. And they don't just magically appear when we become adults. Instead, social skills have to be explicitly taught and practiced in a variety of situations. Although certainly not the only way to do this teaching, Interactive Modeling can be a particularly effective tool in this area.

I witnessed the power of Interactive Modeling when an accreditation team visited my former school. The team wanted to meet with a small group of students to explore the children's school experiences. Eight children from different classes (second through fourth grades) were selected to meet with these unfamiliar adults. As the students entered the room, they confidently greeted each adult, made eye contact, offered a firm handshake, and introduced themselves. During the conversations that followed, the children answered questions succinctly and confidently, looking at all the adults as they did so, not just the adult who had asked the question.

When the children left, the visitors immediately started talking about how advanced these children's social skills were. *How had they developed these essential skills?* The answer, in large part, lay in the school's use of Interactive Modeling. Each of their teachers had used Interactive Modeling to demonstrate a variety of social skills—how to greet someone, how to shake hands, how to make a succinct comment, and how to keep eye contact with one's audience. The children had also had multiple opportunities to practice these skills and receive feedback from their teachers and other school staff.

From these modeling and practice experiences, the students had developed a repertoire of social skills that enabled them to handle a variety of situations with grace and aplomb. Children need these social skills not just to navigate the social aspects of classroom and school life but to excel academically as well. Children who know how to cooperate with others can work productively on group learning projects. Students who develop self-control can sustain attention on academic tasks. Positive social skills lead to stronger academic experiences and increased learning.

In this chapter, you'll learn how you can plan Interactive Modeling lessons to help students develop the social skills they need to succeed in all aspects of their school day.

—— Social Skills and —— Interactive Modeling

✳

The list of social skills children need for school (and for life beyond school) can feel overwhelming. To help make this list more manageable, I cover five broad categories of skills: cooperation, empathy, assertiveness, self-control, and responsibility. Some schools teach a different set of social skills (for example, those based on the work of CASEL, the Collaborative for Academic, Social, and Emotional Learning, which you can learn more about at casel.org). Whichever set of social skills your school or district focuses on, you can adapt the information and examples in this chapter to teach and address those skills.

When we teach children social skills, it's not enough to just go over the big concepts and then remind them to "be caring" or "exercise self-control." Instead, we need to give children a concrete understanding of what it looks and sounds like to translate these concepts into action in various everyday situations. Interactive Modeling is an effective way to do so.

Cooperation

It's essential for students to know how to work well with others—at home, at school, and in the world at large. At school, students must work together on projects, play together at recess, and share tables at lunch. Outside of school, they may play on teams or participate in other group activities. Cooperation is also a critical workplace skill, no matter what career path students take. Examples of skills related to cooperation that can be taught using Interactive Modeling are on the next page.

COOPERATION

- Accept a compliment
- Give a compliment
- Give help when someone asks
- Greet people (classmates, visitors to class, people in hallways)
- Have a friendly, two-way conversation
- Introduce yourself (or two people you know but who don't know each other)
- Make a choice with a partner
- Offer help
- Paraphrase what someone said
- Share information in an interesting and succinct way
- Show appreciation for help, a gift, or a favor
- Wait one's turn (in line, to speak, and so on)

To see how Mrs. Roche, a fourth grade teacher, used Interactive Modeling to teach students how to accept a compliment, see the example that follows.

INTERACTIVE MODELING IN ACTION ✳ **4**th GRADE

10–15 minutes

Accepting a Compliment

1 Say what you will model and why:

Mrs. Roche: "Yesterday, we practiced giving sincere compliments. Today, we're going to learn something that's just as important— how to accept a compliment. That can be hard to do, but it's important that we learn to do it at school as a way to show appreciation and friendliness. I'm going to invite one of you to give me a compliment. Watch and see what I do when I receive it."

2 Model the behavior:

Practicing what she learned the day before, Maria compliments Mrs. Roche, saying, "Mrs. Roche, you're always really cheerful in the morning. That makes it nice to come into the classroom." Mrs. Roche smiles, makes eye contact with Maria, and says, "Thank you, Maria. It makes me feel special to have you notice that about me."

3 Ask students what they noticed:

Mrs. Roche: "What did you notice about how I accepted Maria's compliment?"

Rodney: "You looked at her and said something nice."

Mrs. Roche: [*following up*] "What did I actually say?"

Rodney: "You didn't say it wasn't true—I do that a lot when I get a compliment."

Mrs. Roche: [*acknowledging partial success, prompting for more*] "That's right, I didn't say that; but what *did* I say?"

Rodney: "You said 'thank you' and then told her it made you feel good."

Mrs. Roche: "Why might I say something like that?"

Alize: "You want the person to know that you listened and liked the compliment."

Mrs. Roche: "How did my voice sound when I replied to Maria?"

Ibrahim: "You just sounded normal."

4 Invite one or more students to model:

A shy boy volunteers to model receiving a compliment from Mrs. Roche; she's excited for him to take the spotlight and practice a skill she knows might be hard for him. She asks the students to watch how Patrick accepts her compliment and then says, "Patrick, you write such interesting stories. The one you started yesterday made me laugh out loud." Hesitating, but then sitting up straight and smiling, Patrick says, "Thank you very much. I'm glad you liked my story."

5 Again, ask students what they noticed:

Mrs. Roche: "What did you notice about how Patrick accepted my compliment in a way that showed appreciation and friendliness?"

Selene: "He didn't turn away or look embarrassed."

Mrs. Roche: [*following up*] "What did he do?"

Selene: "He looked you in the eye and smiled. That shows he listened."

Mrs. Roche: "How else did Patrick accept the compliment?"

Samuel: "He thanked you and told you he was glad you liked his story."

Mrs. Roche: "How do you think I felt after he said that?"

Renee: "I think you must have felt glad you said it to him."

6 Have all students practice:

Mrs. Roche: "Now we're all going to practice. Face your partner and take turns giving and accepting compliments. I'll let you know when time is up."

7 Provide feedback:

Mrs. Roche lets the students practice for a few minutes as she mingles, offering positive reinforcement and some specific redirecting to a pair chatting about recess. Then she calls the class back together.

Mrs. Roche: "I saw all of you smiling when you received your compliment, looking at the person, and saying 'thank you.' That's all it takes! What did you notice, especially about how it felt?"

Alize: "At first, it felt strange, but I sort of got used to it."

Samuel: "It felt kind of good to actually know what to say."

Given students' successes, Mrs. Roche tells them that during Friday's closing circle at the end of the day, their job will be to give their partner a compliment and for that person to graciously accept it. The "compliment circle" will become a new class tradition.

• •

To adapt this lesson for younger children:

Give students a context for the compliment. For example: "Let's pretend your partner drew a picture with lots of interesting colors and detail." You might also want to have one more student model, repeating Steps 4 and 5, before having the whole class practice.

Empathy

For some students, being empathetic— understanding things from another person's point of view—is more abstract and challenging than most other social skills. Yet we can teach children what empathy looks  and sounds like in their daily interactions. Carefully constructed Interactive Modeling lessons are a powerful way to do this teaching. Examples of these skills that can be taught using Interactive Modeling are below.

EMPATHY

- Ask a question that reflects genuine interest

- Make an empathetic comment

- Respect personal space

- Respond if someone looks sad or may be hurt

- Take care of someone who goes to time-out

- Take care of someone who loses a game or has a similar setback

- Take care of someone who makes an accidental body noise (see a sample script of this on page 176 in Appendix B)

Assertiveness

Assertiveness is often overlooked and sometimes even discouraged in school, but it's a critical social skill. Students need to be able to assert themselves in respectful and kind (yet firm) ways as they confront the challenges of everyday school life. They need to know how to speak up when they need help, how to let people know what they think or value, how to stand up to someone with whom they disagree or who is behaving unsafely, and how to respectfully balance their needs with those of others. Here are some examples of these skills that can be taught using Interactive Modeling:

ASSERTIVENESS

- Ask for help/make requests
- Decline help if they don't need or want it
- Respectfully disagree (see a sample script of this on page 192 in Appendix B)
- Respond if someone cuts in front of them in line (to get a material, etc.)
- Respond if someone mispronounces their name or calls them the wrong name
- Respond if someone wishes them a happy holiday and they don't celebrate that holiday
- Respond when they can't remember someone's name
- Tell someone to stop doing something that's unsafe or bothering them

How Ms. Rubio, a third grade teacher, taught students what to do if someone called them by the wrong name follows on the next page.

Responding If Someone Calls You the Wrong Name

1 Say what you will model and why:

Ms. Rubio: "Yesterday, we read *The Name Jar* and talked about how important it is to value everyone's names and try our best to pronounce them correctly. It's an important sign of respect to do that. Today, we're going to learn what to do if someone calls you the wrong name. I'm going to ask a volunteer to come up and call me the wrong name. Watch and see what I do."

2 Model the behavior:

Ms. Rubio whispers to Sajo what incorrect name to use. Sajo then comes to the front of the class and says, "Hi, Mrs. Johnson!" Responding with a smile, Ms. Rubio says, "Oops, my name is Ms. Rubio."

3 Ask students what they noticed:

Ms. Rubio: "What did you notice about how I corrected Sajo? How did I follow our rules and take care of myself and her?"

Juan: "You smiled."

Alondra: "You told her the right name."

Ms. Rubio: "How did my face look? How did my voice sound?"

Nicole: "You didn't look or sound mad."

Ms. Rubio: [*following up*] "So how did I look and sound?"

Nicole: "Your face looked normal and happy, and your voice sounded fine, too."

Ms. Rubio: "Why do you think that might be important?"

Henry: "You don't want the other person to feel too embarrassed, so having a regular face is good."

4 Invite one or more students to model:

Katy volunteers to model. Before they begin, Ms. Rubio tells the children that for this and all other "wrong-name" practice, they'll use the name Kermit, which doesn't belong to anyone in the class. She tells the students to notice how Katy corrects her use of the wrong name. In response to her "Good morning, Kermit," Katy smiles and says, "Oh, my name is actually Katy."

5 Again, ask students what they noticed:

Ms. Rubio: "How did Katy let me know her name isn't Kermit without making me feel bad about having called her that?" Students point out Katy's smile, how her face looked friendly, and how she used the word "actually" as a way to sound friendly.

6 Have all students practice:

Ms. Rubio: "Now we're all going to practice. Turn to your partners and take turns asserting yourselves when someone calls you a wrong name—and remember, all our wrong names will be 'Kermit.'"

7 Provide feedback:

Ms. Rubio: [*reinforcing success*] "I saw all of you keeping your sense of humor and smiling at the other person but still being very clear that Kermit was not your name. It's hard to balance taking care of yourself and someone else, but you're learning to do that very well!" Because the students did so well, Ms. Rubio plans to teach a related, but more challenging, assertiveness lesson later that week: what students should do if someone cuts in front of them in line.

● ●

To adapt this lesson for younger children:

Have more than one student model,
repeating Steps 4 and 5.

● ●

To adapt this lesson for older children:

Consider combining it with a lesson on other conversational
mistakes or mistaken assumptions, such as assuming someone
celebrates a certain holiday, and teach how to respectfully
correct the other person's mistake.

Self-Control

Walk through most elementary schools and, within the first five minutes, you're likely to hear a teacher tell students to think about or show some self-control. This is harder than it may seem—self-control (or self-regulation) is actually quite challenging in day-to-day life. That's because we constantly face our own internal impulses and emotions that can cause us to fail to pay attention to others or prompt us to react in impolite, annoying, or even dangerous ways.

As adults, we've had to learn to control our impulses (or find appropriate ways to express them), and this is something we can teach to children. For children, learning self-control will help them get more out of school and of life. They'll be less likely to act disrespectfully and hurt others. And they'll start to understand that by managing their own emotions they can better help others succeed. To teach children what self-control looks and sounds like in many different situations, you can use Interactive Modeling. Here are some examples:

SELF-CONTROL

- Accept "no" as an answer
- Calm down
- Clap politely
- Go directly to time-out
- Refrain from calling out or making a comment when someone else is speaking
- Sit still during a read-aloud

- Show excitement or other strong emotions without disturbing others or calling too much attention to themselves
- Talk quietly, even when excited
- Walk, not run
- Wait for a turn in a game, at the water fountain, in line, and so on

---

Note: Many of the sample scripts in Appendix B, starting on page 174, also help reinforce self-control or can be adapted to teach these skills.

Responsibility

How can we teach children to do the tasks they're assigned, to admit when they've made a mistake, and to act safely to ensure that no one gets hurt? In other words, how do we teach children to be responsible? Through Interactive Modeling, we can give students a set of real-life skills that responsible people use day in and day out. Here are some examples:

RESPONSIBILITY

- Admit that they made a mistake
- Acknowledge that they broke something
- Apologize
- Blow their nose, sneeze, and cough in ways that are polite and healthy for all

- Pick up trash and throw it away
- Put belongings away neatly
- Tell an adult if someone is hurt

How Mr. Lopez, a first grade teacher, used Interactive Modeling to teach students a way to apologize follows on the next page.

10 minutes

Apologizing

1 Say what you will model and why:

Mr. Lopez: "As we discussed yesterday, if we do something mean or dis-
respectful, it causes hurt. When that happens, there are some
things we can do to help the person feel better. One way to do
that is to apologize. Watch what I say and do."

2 Model the behavior:

Tony volunteers to model with Mr. Lopez. Looking Tony in the eye,
Mr. Lopez says in a sincere tone, "I am very sorry that I said you
couldn't sit with me at lunch. I was not being a good friend. I hope
you can forgive me."

3 Ask students what they noticed:

Mr. Lopez: "What did you notice about how I tried to give my apology
in a way that would help Tony feel better?"

Amber: "You apologized."

Emilio: "You told him why it was bad."

Mr. Lopez: [*prompting for specifics*] "Do you remember some of the
words that I used?" The children offer a few.

Mr. Lopez: [*prompting for important details the children haven't stated*]
"How did my face look?" "Where were my eyes looking?"
"How did my voice sound?"

Amaya: "Your face was serious, and you looked right at Tony." Other
children answer with the details Mr. Lopez expected them
to notice.

Mr. Lopez: [*emphasizing an important point*] "What did I say about why I was mean?" The children look a little surprised at this question. Mr. Lopez gives them think time.

Colin: "Nothing?"

Mr. Lopez: "That's right. When we apologize, we can just say that we're sorry. We don't have to try to explain or excuse what we did."

4 Invite one or more students to model:

Satisfied that the children are starting to understand the complexities of this simple model, Mr. Lopez invites Rossina to model apologizing to him in the same way that he apologized to Tony.

5 Again, ask students what they noticed:

Mr. Lopez: "How did Rossina give her apology to try to help me feel better?" Students point out all the important specific behaviors.

Knowing that apologizing is a challenging social skill to master, Mr. Lopez asks for one more student volunteer before the whole group practices.

6 Have all students practice:

Mr. Lopez: "It's time for everyone to practice. Turn to your partner and take turns giving an apology for saying he or she can't sit with you at lunch."

7 Provide feedback:

After mingling with as many pairs as he can, Mr. Lopez reinforces the entire group.

Mr. Lopez: "I saw all of you looking each other in the eye and using a kind, sincere voice. It sounded like you really meant what you said. You all said you were sorry without giving any excuses. You're off to a good start with knowing how to apologize!"

For the next few days, when Mr. Lopez notices children having small disputes, he prompts them to think whether an apology might help. He also finds opportunities during the day to ask the class, "What have you noticed about how we're doing with apologizing? Has anyone offered you an apology? How did it feel?" Later, he follows up this lesson with one on how to respond respectfully to an apology.

● ●

To adapt this lesson for older children:

If you think older students have experience with apologies, consider using role-play to teach them these skills.

—— Tips for Success With —— Social Skills

*

Visualize exactly how a social situation should be handled.

This can be challenging because sometimes we aren't sure ourselves of the best way to handle certain social situations, or we may struggle in a given area. I know that when I teach assertiveness skills, I often have to do a little research to figure out respectful ways to say "no" or to disagree because I never really fully developed these skills.

Also, be careful not just to accept how social situations are typically handled. For instance, both children and adults often accept apologies by saying, "That's OK." While intended to be gracious, this acceptance falls short because when someone has hurt us, it's really *not* OK. We can certainly choose to accept the apology, but we don't want to condone the behavior by saying, "That's OK." A better way to teach children how to accept an apology would be to model saying, "I forgive you" or "I accept your apology." When in doubt about the most appropriate way to handle a social situation, consult with colleagues or do some reading on the topic.

Remember to model only positive behaviors.

When teaching how to handle difficult situations or strong emotions, it can be tempting to show a negative behavior in an attempt to dramatize or emphasize a key point. For example, in teaching students how to respond if someone does something that upsets them, it may seem worthwhile to act out the knocking over of a tower of blocks or the use of rude language, but don't give in to this impulse. The advice I gave in Chapter 1, page 23, still holds in these teaching situations: model only positive behaviors.

Have a clear learning goal.

It may seem obvious, but take the time to clarify exactly what you want children to learn to do. This way, your lesson will be more focused and, as a result, more effective. The learning goal should specifically describe the behavior children will be able to exhibit as a result of the lesson. For instance, if you want to teach an Interactive Modeling lesson on how to share information, the learning goal might be: "Students will be able to share on a given topic in a clear, succinct, and interesting way, speaking at an appropriate volume and making eye contact with listeners." Explicitly defining the goal will help you—and, more importantly, your students—clearly understand the social skill you're teaching.

Use other adults or older students to help model when appropriate.

Social skills involve interactions with others, so it's helpful to show students what these skills look like by using two or more adult or older students as models. For instance, when modeling how to talk with someone at lunch on a given topic, students may develop a stronger vision of what these conversational skills look like if they see competent adults or older students modeling. When possible, recruit fellow teachers, paraprofessionals, other colleagues, and capable older students to model with you, especially for any social skills that involve particularly challenging social situations.

Don't expect perfection.

You'll need to give students some time before expecting the social skills covered in this chapter to become automatic, just as you need to give them time to master reading, math, and other academic skills. Most social skills are complex, so children will need frequent and low-key practice, positive reinforcement, and effective coaching to develop these skills. Be patient as children learn and make mistakes—and remember that many adults struggle with these very same social skills!

Make sure Interactive Modeling fits.

Remember that Interactive Modeling is designed for a situation in which there is one specific way that students should do something. Because many situations in the social arena are much more complex, consider other teaching strategies as a way to reinforce your initial lesson or as an alternative way of teaching the skill. For example, children need to learn multiple ways to approach other children and ask them to play or sit together at lunch. Role-play, as noted on page 23, is a useful strategy to help students learn how to handle those situations.

A gray area exists between Interactive Modeling and role-play, however. With younger children, I sometimes use Interactive Modeling for a skill like how to give a compliment even though I would use role-play with older students. But even older students may lack the experiences or language skills to participate meaningfully in role-play. In these situations, use Interactive Modeling to help students first learn some basic skills and then start to help them build a repertoire of more complex skills with additional modeling or role-play.

Adapt the lessons in this chapter for older students as needed.

Don't dismiss Interactive Modeling as a strategy for older students. Often, they need as much work developing social skills as younger children do. Of course, if you see that students have already mastered a skill, such as taking turns, you needn't do a separate lesson on it. For skills that older students still need to develop or practice, take into account their developmental needs, abilities, and interests in your planning. Choose situations and ways of behaving that would seem realistic and appropriate to them. Use sophisticated language geared to their ability levels, even if the concept or skill is relatively simplistic.

Also, find ways to make the lessons directly relevant to their lives and interests whenever you can. For instance, after teaching students the art of giving and accepting apologies, you could bring in current or historical apologies and have students analyze whether and how they matched up to what they learned.

Consider the diversity of children's cultural backgrounds.

We all need to be aware of and sensitive to cultural differences in the classroom. What's considered a useful social skill in one culture might not be in another. For example, in some cultures, making eye contact is a sign of disrespect, and approaching and speaking to adults without their speaking first may also be considered impolite. Yet we still need to prepare students to be successful within and across cultures. If you have certain social expectations that might conflict with children's home cultures, present those expectations as ones that are important for success in school.

Reinforce success.

Making students aware of their progress and positive behaviors in the social arena helps them develop and master a set of social skills that will enable them to become successful students and adults. Remember to avoid giving students general "Good job!" praise. Instead, let your appreciation for their acts of caring, kindness, and responsibility shine through by carefully observing and describing what you notice throughout the school day.

——— A Closing Thought ———

We frequently use aspirational terms to describe the kinds of people we want students to become: caring, responsible, empathetic, cooperative, and ethical. These are worthy goals, but to make them a reality, we need to break these broad concepts down into smaller, attainable, concrete behaviors and skills. Interactive Modeling allows us to do just that.

Points to Remember

✳

→ *Think about the social skills students need to be successful at school.* Prioritize which skills you need to teach first.

→ *Connect social skills to specific rules and learning goals.*

→ *Break complex skills into bite-sized pieces.*

→ *Focus on progress, not perfection.*

→ *Reteach social skills, especially after long breaks away from school.*

→ *Reinforce success often.* Focus on the positives you see and the progress students are making.

• • • • • • • • • •

For more help using Interactive Modeling to teach social skills, use the Planning Guide and Timelines in Appendix A, pages 169–173.

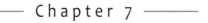

Chapter 7

When to Do Abbreviated Interactive Modeling

I n the Introduction, I encouraged you to stick to the seven-step Inter-active Modeling format as you learn to use it. However, as you hone your skills and your students hone theirs, you may want to abbreviate your Interactive Modeling in some situations. In this chapter, I'll address several of these situations and give you ideas for how to do an abbreviated Interactive Modeling lesson.

——— Building on Previous ———
Teaching

✳

Often, children develop new skills by first mastering a simple skill and then either slowly adding complexities or varying how they use that skill. For instance, students might first learn to respond to a chime as a signal for quiet attention, and later learn to respond to other nonverbal signals, such as a raised hand for quiet attention or a rewind signal to back up and make a point more respectfully. So if you have done several previous Interactive Modeling lessons focused on the same area of skills or behaviors, you may be able to shorten or modify later lessons.

I often used Interactive Modeling to teach children various handshakes for use in group greetings, such as a traditional handshake, a high five, and a fist bump. After doing full Interactive Modeling lessons on these handshakes, I could often teach other, more complicated variations using an abbreviated modeling format. I would model the new handshake and have students notice key aspects, perhaps comparing those to prior handshakes. Then I could turn it over to them to practice, bypassing the usual next step of having one or two students model.

——— When Students Are ———
Experienced With
Interactive Modeling

✳

As the school year goes on, you may decide that you need to do only the first few steps of Interactive Modeling. By the spring, if you have been using Interactive Modeling lessons frequently (and your students have become adept at their role), you may be able to teach completely new skills just by demonstrating them, having students point out important aspects of what you did, and practicing themselves.

For instance, I taught a few variations of tag to my students at recess. At the beginning of the year, I often used all the steps of Interactive Modeling to teach these variations. Then as the year went on and students became more adept at noticing and modeling for themselves, I could use the abbreviated form to teach new playground games that included a whole new set of skills.

Reteaching

Have you ever returned weeks later to an academic skill or concept that you thoroughly taught—and thought your students had mastered—only to discover that they seemed to have no memory of it? Despite the best initial teaching, students sometimes need us to reteach concepts or skills. Certain situations or times of the day, week, or year can also upset even well-established behaviors, skills, and routines. And sometimes students, as a group or individually, just need more support.

In each of these situations, students can greatly benefit from a refresher and more guided practice using an abbreviated Interactive Modeling format. The following are some common situations for reteaching, along with suggestions for how to do it.

Before and after breaks (and other special events)

Any disruption to the usual daily schedule can cause students to stumble, forgetting rules and expectations. They may simply be overly excited or tired, or they may have gotten used to a different routine if away from school. These are times to reteach proactively—before students have a chance to show you they've forgotten. Some productive times to do this reteaching are:

- ➤ Monday mornings

- ➤ Tuesday mornings after a three-day weekend

- ➤ Friday afternoons

- ➤ Right before and right after a long school break

- ➤ Before and after a substitute teacher or guest speaker

- ➤ When a new student joins the class

- ➤ Before assemblies and field trips

Sometimes to reteach, you may want to go through all the steps of Interactive Modeling again, depending upon your class and the time you have. Most often, though, using an abbreviated version is all that's needed for reteaching to be successful.

Consider a sixth grade teacher, Ms. Merkel. At the beginning of the year, she uses a complete Interactive Modeling lesson to teach her students how to show that they're listening, signal agreement, and use conversational phrases, such as *I want to agree with*, *disagree with*, *add on to*, and *what _____ said*. Then, after every school break, Ms. Merkel does a quick re-modeling lesson to remind students of these expectations. That's because she knows they may forget the expectations for class discussions and that these can differ from expectations at home. Her students generally understand and have lived up to expectations, so Ms. Merkel wants to convey her recognition of their skills while also giving a gentle reminder and vision of what those expectations should look like in action. She knows that an abbreviated form of Interactive Modeling should serve these purposes very well.

As you read Ms. Merkel's abbreviated Interactive Modeling lesson on the next page, see how she uses the first step of the lesson to invite student input. Also, notice that rather than doing the modeling herself, she has a small group of students model.

ABBREVIATED INTERACTIVE MODELING LESSON for Reteaching Classroom Discussion Expectations With the Whole Class	
Steps	**What I Will Say and Do**
a Tell students what will be modeled and why (or ask them for the "why").	"Our class rules say we will take care of ourselves and each other. What do you remember about how we do those things during classroom discussions, and why do they matter?"
b Ask one or more students to model the behavior you are reteaching (choose those you've noticed meeting expectations).	"Andre, Jose, DeAna, and Parker, join me up front. We'll have a discussion about whether our cafeteria should change food vendors. Andre, you start. I'll call on the other three students as they show the signal we've practiced. Everyone else, watch and see what you notice."
c Ask what students noticed.	"What did you notice these four do to take care of each other as they discussed the topic?"
d Have all students practice.	"I'm going to open up the conversation to everyone. Let's all practice showing interested listening, signaling agreement, and using our conversational phrases."
e Provide specific feedback.	"I saw people looking at the person speaking and waiting until that person finished, even though you wanted to add something to the conversation. I saw lots of people showing agreement, and still others respectfully disagreeing by saying, 'I disagree with so and so because. . . .' It looks like we're ready to have more of these safe conversations, just as we did before the break."

When you first notice students are forgetting

At times, you may see clues that your class needs you to reteach an Inter-active Modeling lesson. Maybe they're beginning to slip with the cafeteria routine, leaving tables a little messier or raising their speaking volume higher than you had taught. The best time to revisit an Interactive Modeling lesson is at the first sign that students are forgetting some key aspects. Don't wait until they've gone completely off track! Depending on what you observe, you can adapt the abbreviated lesson for a whole class (see below) or for an individual student or small group (see page 160).

For example, in Chapter 2, pages 42–44, you read the Interactive Modeling lesson Mr. O'Grady did with second graders about using polite manners in the cafeteria. One Wednesday, Mr. O'Grady sat in at lunch to see how students were doing. He noticed that some were talking while chewing, others interrupted classmates who were speaking, and a few weren't staying in their seats.

As a result of what he observed, he decided to do a whole-class abbreviated Interactive Modeling lesson the next day to reteach expectations for cafeteria behavior. You can read this lesson below. Note that Mr. O'Grady decided to skip the usual Step 2 (model the behavior yourself) and Step 3 (ask students what they saw you do) because time was limited and he knew that students had previously encountered a long period of success with meeting expectations. They just needed a little help refocusing and a bit more practice.

You can adapt this abbreviated Interactive Modeling lesson for any whole-group reteaching you need to do. (This structure can also be used with small groups.)

ABBREVIATED INTERACTIVE MODELING LESSON **for Reteaching Lunch Table Behaviors With the Whole Class**	
Steps	**What I Will Say and Do**
a Tell students what will be modeled and why (or ask them for the "why").	"Our class rules say we will take care of ourselves and each other. What does that mean for how we act at the lunch table?"

Steps	What I Will Say and Do
b Ask one or more students to model the behavior you are reteaching (choose those you've noticed meeting expectations).	"Anika, can you show us how we practiced sitting in one spot and eating lunch appropriately? Everyone else, watch and see what you notice."
c Ask what students noticed.	"What did you notice Anika do to take care of herself and other people?"
d Have all students practice.	"I'm going to visit lunch today and see everyone practice how to sit in one spot and eat lunch appropriately."
e Provide specific feedback.	"I saw people staying in one spot at lunch today and eating their food. I saw mouths closed as you chewed, and the cafeteria staff noticed how calm and happy your lunch was today!"

When one student or a few students are struggling

Sometimes, most of your students may be following expectations for given behaviors, routines, or skills, but you notice that a small group or an individual is struggling. Perhaps they just need more practice. Or maybe they are developmentally older or younger than the other children.

For example, most of your students may have successfully mastered keeping their desks and materials organized, but organization may still be a challenge for some. You might want to remodel for these students and even provide some additional support (such as posting a visual reminder of what the desk should look like or doing a daily desk check for a week). Or perhaps you taught students how to give a succinct book talk, but some continue to give too much detail. Consider pulling those students together for an abbreviated remodeling lesson and additional practice so you can give them more individual feedback and coaching.

For your reteaching, choose a time of day that will feel natural to students, not punitive. For example, if a student is struggling with putting away supplies, try reteaching just before or after the work time with those supplies. It's best not to do reteaching by taking time out of children's recess or other free time (unless the struggles are related to those). Treat the small group or individual session just as you would if you were reteaching an acdemic concept—and keep it positive!

Here's an example of an Interactive Modeling lesson for reteaching with an individual student or small group. Note that the usual Step 4 (invite one or more students to model) and Step 5 (again, ask students what they noticed) are not used.

ABBREVIATED INTERACTIVE MODELING LESSON for Reteaching the Signal for Quiet Attention With an Individual Student or Small Group	
Steps	**What I Will Say and Do**
a Tell the student (or small group) what you'll be modeling and why (or ask for the "why").	"When I ring the chime, you need to give me your attention quickly and safely. This helps everyone be ready to learn."
b Model the behavior yourself.	"You pretend to be me and ring the chime. Then watch what I do. See what you notice."
c Ask the student what she or he noticed.	"What did you notice about how I responded to the signal?"
d Have the student practice.	"Now I want you to respond to the signal in the same way I just did."
e Provide specific feedback.	"That only took you two seconds. Your voice was turned off, you looked at me, and your hands were still. I'm going to ring the chime in about five minutes for the whole class. I bet you can do this again."

Always keep in mind that any behavior, skill, or routine takes time and practice to master—and some of us need more time and practice to learn new things than others do. Think of how much time and practice most children need to learn how to clean their room independently, say "please" and "thank you" automatically, or take responsibility for homework and other chores on their own. You may need to reteach certain Interactive Modeling lessons several times, but that doesn't mean that you or the children have failed. It only means they need more time for positive habits to truly settle in and solidify.

When You've Retaught, but Students Are Still Struggling

✳

Recently, I worked with a first grade teacher who wanted help with the class's independent work time. She expected her first graders to work silently for thirty to forty minutes. I knew that she had done a strong Interactive Modeling lesson and a great deal of follow-up practice. Yet students were still having difficulty meeting this expectation.

I asked her to take another look at what she expected these young children to be able to do. Then we discussed how hard it is for any group to work silently for a long stretch of time, especially first graders, who developmentally tend to be talkative. She concluded that her expectations for children were the stumbling blocks, not her modeling or the children themselves.

Children sometimes struggle not because they need more reteaching or practice, but because our expectations may be unrealistic. At times, we may overshoot and expect more than children are capable of doing comfortably. At other times, we might make procedures so complicated that even children with advanced skills can't remember all the steps.

If students are consistently struggling with a given routine or behavior, despite a well-planned initial modeling lesson, repeated practice, and reteaching, take a step back. Ask yourself if your expectations are realistic:

➤ Is the behavior developmentally appropriate?

➤ Is the routine or skill too complex?

➤ Are there too many steps for children to remember?

➤ Is something else getting in the way of children's learning?

When you analyze your expectations from a fresh perspective, you'll be more likely to make changes that will better ensure students' success.

Here are some ways to go about analyzing what might be preventing the children from succeeding:

Rethink your space or routines.

Our setup of a routine or physical space can tax students in ways that not even the best Interactive Modeling lesson can overcome. For instance, is your class having trouble lining up quietly and safely in the classroom? Perhaps how the furniture is arranged makes getting in a line too challenging. Or maybe there are too many distractions near the door. Sometimes transitions are rough because students have to return materials to one spot all at the same time. If this is the case in your classroom, could you modify the routine or storage system to prevent logjams? Some teachers do a walk-through with an eye to seeing where the physical stumbling blocks are and how they can be resolved.

Videotape yourself teaching an Interactive Modeling lesson.

As you watch the video, consider your pace. Are you moving so slowly that students aren't staying engaged? Are you going so quickly that students don't have time to internalize the behaviors? Are you calling attention to the most important aspects of what you're teaching? Are your students pointing out what *to* do, rather than what *not* to do? Review and analyze your lessons with questions like these in mind.

Have a colleague observe and give you feedback.

Sometimes it takes another person's viewpoint to give us insight into where our teaching has gone off track. If you can, seek a colleague who understands Interactive Modeling and uses it successfully. Ask him or her to observe a lesson or two and give you a little coaching. If your colleague can record exactly what you say and do, it will also help you analyze your teaching—for example, whether your opening statement was succinct and your modeling was clear. Another option is to ask a colleague to teach the class for a few minutes while you observe, to see if you notice things that might be causing children to stumble.

Consider whether students are receiving sufficient feedback.

It's not realistic to expect children to master certain behaviors or skills without having chances to practice and hear how they're doing. They may do really well when they practice during the initial lesson, but if we fail to notice and reinforce their subsequent efforts and successes, they'll likely slip back into old habits.

With our days so hectic, it's easy to forget to give positive reminders and respectful redirections when students start to go off track. As a result, the impact of our Interactive Modeling can start to fade away. Whenever students are trying to apply the lessons of your Interactive Modeling, remember to coach them.

To help you remember to reinforce or respectfully remind students, consider these tips:

- ➤ Post sentence starters ("I notice . . . I see . . . I hear . . . You all did . . .") where you can see them. One of my former colleagues, a music teacher, displayed pictures of composers—each with a sentence starter inside a speech bubble.

- ➤ Write some sample language directly into your lesson plans or on a sticky note. Doing so will remind you to use that language and have it ready when you need it.

➤ Set a reminder on your phone, computer, or other device to go off at certain times. When you hear it, find something positive (and specific) to reinforce with the whole group, a small group, or an individual.

➤ Regularly send home notes to individual students highlighting successes you've observed.

➤ If you teach older students, tell them you're working on giving more positive feedback and assign one of them a class job of keeping track of when you do so.

Ask students what they think the problem may be.

Children often have a great deal of insight into what has gone wrong with a particular part of their day. If they're struggling with a behavior or skill that you think is appropriate to expect of them and you have taught well, consider asking your students where things are going awry. Be sure to phrase this as an open-ended question with genuine curiosity so that you can get truly meaningful feedback.

For instance, after pointing out to the class that you have noticed children are coming back late from recess, you might ask, "What are some strategies you could use to help make sure you line up when you hear the whistle?" or "What ideas do you have for solving this problem?" Or, if you hear from the custodian that students are not following the bathroom routines you taught, you might say, "How can we remember to take care of the bathrooms? How can we remind each other to do so?"

—— A Closing Thought ——

Like any teaching technique, Interactive Modeling is most effective when you tailor it to students' needs and abilities, which may ebb and flow over the course of the school year. As you decide when and how to abbreviate an Interactive Modeling lesson, consider the complexity of the behavior or skill and the developmental levels of the children. Remember to refer often to this chapter and Chapter 1 for guidance.

Points to Remember

✳

➤ *Use abbreviated Interactive Modeling as students develop skills and become more adept with Interactive Modeling.*

➤ *Be proactive.* Plan to reteach at certain times or as soon as you see signs that students are struggling.

➤ *Keep the reteaching positive, not punitive.*

➤ *Remodel and provide extra support for students who still struggle.*

➤ *Continue to reinforce positive behaviors.*

• • • • • • • • • •

For more help creating effective abbreviated Interactive Modeling lessons, use the Planning Guide and Timelines in Appendix A, pages 169–173.

Afterword

I always find it helpful to keep in mind that the goal of Interactive Modeling isn't compliance, but cooperation. Even though Interactive Modeling is very effective when we need students to do something in one specific way, it's not intended to create a "my way or the highway" classroom environment or learning mentality. That's why it's so important to focus on what our students are doing well and the improvements we see.

Progress, not perfection, should be the goal of any teaching practice. If Interactive Modeling does not feel natural to you at first or does not go exactly the way you had hoped, step back a bit. Take a slow, deep breath and let yourself have a little time to think about what *has* gone well.

From experience, I know that Interactive Modeling does lead to successful learning for children. It's a straightforward technique that has greater and greater impact the more we develop our skills in using it. And the only way to develop those skills is to make mistakes, reflect on them, and try again. I hope you will embrace your mistakes and the self-learning that results.

So give Interactive Modeling a try, be patient, plan lessons carefully, reflect on how they went, and adjust as needed. Once you do, you'll discover that this simple teaching practice can set you and your students up for success every day and across the curriculum—and enable all of you to do great things in school.

Planning Guide and Timelines

E ven if you've done lots of Interactive Modeling with your students, planning each lesson will help maximize its potential for success and ensure that the children get the most out of it. When planning to teach an Interactive Modeling lesson, think about questions like these:

→ Why is this behavior or skill important?

→ What's the learning goal for students—that is, what do you want them to be able to do as a result of the lesson?

→ How will you introduce the lesson?

→ What exactly will you model?

→ What details do you want students to notice?

→ How will you coach students as they practice? What things might go wrong and how will you respond if they do?

→ What materials or additional support (if any) do you need?

→ How will you follow up with this lesson?

Use the Planning Guide on the next page to help you prepare your lessons. The Timelines on pages 171–173 can also help you plan a rough schedule of what to teach using Interactive Modeling (and when) during the school year.

Interactive Modeling Planning Guide

Behavior/Skill to Model: _____

Steps	Think about ...	What will you actually do and say as you model and coach?
1 Say what you will model and why.	• Why is this behavior or skill important to students and the classroom community? • Which classroom rule(s) are relevant?	
2 Model the behavior.	• What particular aspects of this behavior or skill are important to show explicitly?	
3 Ask students what they noticed.	• What specific details are students *not* likely to mention? How might you coach students to notice these details?	
4 Have one or more students model the same behavior.	• How many volunteer(s) will you need? How will you select them? • Will you need to practice with the volunteer(s) beforehand?	
5 Again, ask students what they noticed.	• What specific details are students *not* likely to mention? How might you coach students to notice these details?	
6 Have all students practice.	• How will students practice? How can you make practice engaging? • Will all students practice immediately or will you need to space it out over a day or two?	
7 Provide feedback.	• How will you point out students' successes? • How might students get off track? How might you remind or redirect them ?	

Reflections:

Sample Interactive Modeling Timelines

Here are examples of how you might schedule Interactive Modeling lessons throughout the year for various aspects of the school day:

Grades K–2 Timeline		
	Weeks 1–2	Weeks 3–8	Weeks 9– end of year
What do children in the early elementary grades need to learn to be successful as they start off in school? Notes:	☐ Routines (morning meeting, bathroom, snack, recess, lunch)	☐ Routines (classroom library, reading/writing workshops, math/science centers)	☐ Routines (new procedures for centers or workshops, new recess games)
	☐ Transitions (arrival and dismissal, to and from circle)	☐ Transitions (among centers, during workshops)	☐ Transitions (new or revised)
	☐ Using and caring for basic materials (pencils, markers, simple math manipulatives, books)	☐ Using and caring for intermediate materials (technology, art materials, content area supplies)	☐ Using and caring for complex materials (new software, science equipment)
	☐ Social skills (taking turns, sharing materials)	☐ Social skills (sharing ideas, apologizing, giving compliments)	☐ Social skills (disagreeing, asserting an opinion, reacting with respect if upset)
	☐ Academic skills (talking with a partner, using a word wall for help with spelling)	☐ Academic skills (reading with a partner, asking questions, new content area skills)	☐ Academic skills (deciding what is important in a text, giving feedback to peers, new content area skills)

Remember to reteach after breaks!

Grades 3–4 Timeline		
	Weeks 1–2	**Weeks 3–8**	**Weeks 9– end of year**
What do children in the middle elementary grades need to learn to be successful— now that they're a little more experienced in school? Notes:	☐ Routines (morning meeting, bathroom, recess, lunch, reading/writing workshops)	☐ Routines (individual projects, class jobs, homework)	☐ Routines (group work and projects, student-led recess games)
	☐ Transitions (arrival and dismissal, from instruction to independent work)	☐ Transitions (during workshops, to and from project work)	☐ Transitions (new or revised)
	☐ Using and caring for basic materials (math manipulatives, folders/ binders, basic technology)	☐ Using and caring for intermediate materials (science equipment, intermediate technology)	☐ Using and caring for complex materials (new software or equipment)
	☐ Social skills (conversation skills, presenting information, asking questions)	☐ Social skills (apologizing, giving compliments, respectfully disagreeing, making pertinent comments)	☐ Social skills (paraphrasing what someone said, making I-statements, reaching a compromise)
	☐ Academic skills (talking with a partner, giving feedback to a partner, heading one's paper)	☐ Academic skills (recording observations, using graphic organizers, new content area skills)	☐ Academic skills (test prep skills, taking notes, new content area skills)

Remember to reteach after breaks!

Grades 5–6 Timeline			
	Weeks 1–2	**Weeks 3–8**	**Weeks 9– end of year**
What do children in the later elementary grades need to learn to be successful as they complete elementary school and prepare for middle school? Notes:	☐ Routines (student-led recess games, bathroom, lunch, reading/writing workshops, individual projects, homework)	☐ Routines (group projects, cross-grade buddies, schoolwide jobs such as flag duty)	☐ Routines (research projects, leadership roles)
	☐ Transitions (arrival and dismissal, from instruction to independent work, during workshops and project time)	☐ Transitions (new or revised)	☐ Transitions (walking to and from classes without supervision to move towards independence)
	☐ Using and caring for basic materials (textbooks, folders/binders, basic technology)	☐ Using and caring for intermediate materials (science equipment, intermediate technology)	☐ Using and caring for complex materials (new software or equipment)
	☐ Social skills (asking questions, making empathetic comments, apologizing, giving and receiving compliments)	☐ Social skills (making formal presentations, paraphrasing what others said, respectfully disagreeing)	☐ Social skills (making I-statements, reaching a compromise, interviewing adults for research/other projects)
	☐ Academic skills (giving feedback to a partner, locating/highlighting important information in a text, basic content area skills)	☐ Academic skills (taking notes, using graphic organizers, study skills, new content area skills)	☐ Academic skills (test prep skills, new content area skills)

Remember to reteach after breaks!

Sample Scripts

INTERACTIVE MODELING FOR GRADES K–2

10 minutes

How to Sit and Show Listening in the Circle

Steps	What It Might Sound/Look Like
1 Say what you will model and why.	"To learn, we all need to listen. I'm going to show you what listening looks like on the rug. Watch what I do."
2 Model the behavior.	Without talking, show how to sit down at a spot on the rug: legs crossed, hands in lap, back straight, facing the teacher's chair, and leaning slightly toward it. Then smile and nod a little to show attentive listening.
3 Ask students what they noticed.	"What did I do to show I was listening?" If necessary, follow up with specific questions to prompt children to list the key aspects of the behavior. For example: "What was my mouth doing? Did you notice what my hands were doing? What about my legs and feet? How did I show that I was really paying attention?"
4 Invite one or more students to model.	"Who can show us how to listen the way I showed you?" After a student volunteers, give a simple direction. For example: "Watch Angela. See how she sits and listens."
5 Again, ask students what they noticed.	"How did Angela sit and listen?" As needed, elicit from children that Angela was looking at the teacher chair, sitting with her legs crossed, and nodding and smiling. Repeat Steps 4 and 5 to reinforce learning if needed.
6 Have all students practice.	"Now let's see if we all can show how to sit and listen the way Angela and I did."
7 Provide feedback.	Offer your observations in a warm, but not gushing, tone. For example: "That's it! You all did exactly what we showed. You were sitting up straight with your legs crossed. You had your hands in your lap and your eyes on me. Lots of you were smiling and nodding. It looks like we are ready to learn together. Let's read a book and see how we do with our listening."

INTERACTIVE MODELING FOR GRADES K–2

10 minutes

What to Do If Someone Makes an Accidental Body Noise

Note: Before doing this lesson, the teacher read *The Gas We Pass* by Shinta Cho aloud to the class to help them start to understand the importance of empathy.

Steps	What It Might Sound/Look Like
1 **Say what you will model and why.**	"Yesterday, we read the book *The Gas We Pass* and talked about how all of us sometimes have to do that, even at school. Our rules say that we will take care of each other, so we need to take care of anyone who accidentally passes gas at school. Let's pretend that it's read-aloud time and our stuffed animal, Mudge, just passed gas. Watch and see what I do."
2 **Model the behavior.**	Have a volunteer be the teacher and read aloud from a book or morning message chart. Have another volunteer stand by the stuffed animal and make a sound to represent someone passing gas. (**Note:** To avoid silliness, consider what you know about your students and decide on the actual noise in advance.) When the noise happens, show how to keep your eyes on the person reading and maintain the same facial expression.
3 **Ask students what they noticed.**	"What did you notice about how I took care of Mudge when he passed gas?" If necessary, ask follow-up questions such as "How did my face look? Where were my eyes looking? Why does it matter that I stayed focused on the book and kept my face the same?"
4 **Invite one or more students to model.**	"Who could show us how to take good care of Mudge when he passes gas, just as I did?"
5 **Again, ask students what they noticed.**	"How did Kara take care of Mudge?" Encourage students to point out specific behaviors.
6 **Have all students practice.**	"Now we're all going to practice. Allie will start reading a poem, we'll hear the noise [the teacher should make the noise], and then we'll all take care of whoever did it."
7 **Provide feedback.**	"I saw all of you continue to look at and listen to Allie. Everyone's face stayed the same. It looks as if we're going to take good care of each other should this happen to one of us."

INTERACTIVE MODELING FOR GRADES K–2

15 minutes

Walking Safely and Quietly in the Hallway

Steps	What It Might Sound/Look Like
1 Say what you will model and why.	"This year in kindergarten, we'll need to go to lots of places in the school. We'll need to get there safely and quietly, so other people in our school can stay focused on their learning. Ms. Carrera, Mr. Allen, and I are going to show you what it looks and sounds like to walk in line. Watch and see how we do that."
2 Model the behavior.	Walk in line around the room, being especially careful to keep a steady pace, maintain a close but safe distance while walking, and keep eyes forward, hands to self, and voices off.
3 Ask students what they noticed.	"What did you notice about how we walked in line?"
	If necessary, follow up with questions such as "What did you notice about how far I was from Ms. Carrera? What were my hands doing? Where did I keep my eyes? What was my voice doing?"
4 Invite one or more students to model.	"Who can show us how to walk in line the same way we did?" After choosing volunteer models, give a simple direction: "Watch how Elena and Patrice walk in line."
5 Again, ask students what they noticed.	"How did Elena and Patrice show us safe and quiet walking in line?"
6 Have all students practice.	"Now we're going to play a game to practice walking in line. When you hear the music, you'll walk the same way we all did. I'll watch to see how you do. When the music stops, freeze just the way we practiced this morning, and then I'll tell you what I saw."
7 Provide feedback.	"Wow, you've got it! You all kept up with each other at a good pace, stayed close but not too close to each other, and were quiet. Your hands were at your sides, and you paid close attention to the person in front of you. Let's try again!"

Note: Giving students something to do or think about when they practice actually walking in the hallway can also be helpful. For example, they could look for shapes, numbers, or objects that start with a certain letter.

INTERACTIVE MODELING FOR GRADES K–2

10–15 minutes

Dismissal Routine
(getting backpacks and gathering in a circle before dismissal)

Steps	What It Might Sound/Look Like
1 **Say what you will model and why.**	"A little later, it's going to be time to leave school. I'll show you how to do that so we can have a happy ending to our day. I'm going to pretend that my teacher has just told us to get our backpacks and come to the circle. Watch and see how I take care of myself, my classmates, and my backpack."
2 **Model the behavior.**	In advance, ask a child if you can use her backpack. Walk straight over to the cubby, pick up the backpack, and walk back to the circle. When you arrive at your spot, carefully place the backpack behind your spot. Sit down and look at where the teacher would be sitting.
3 **Ask students what they noticed.**	"What did you see me do?" If necessary, follow up with questions such as "How did I get from here to the cubbies? How did I carry the backpack? How did I move on my way back? Where did I put the back-pack when I got to the circle? What did I do with my body once I had my backpack behind me?"
4 **Invite one or more students to model.**	"Who can show us how to go get his or her backpack the same exact way I did?"
5 **Again, ask students what they noticed.**	"What did you see Sophie do?" Possible follow-up: "How did Sophie take care of herself, other people, and her backpack?"
6 **Have all students practice.**	Repeat Steps 4 and 5 with small groups until everyone has had a turn.
7 **Provide feedback.**	Reinforce each group after they return: "You all walked to get your backpacks, carried them safely, and came right back. You put them down behind you and sat down. Way to go!"

INTERACTIVE MODELING FOR GRADES **K–2**

5–10 minutes

How to Use and Store Glue Sticks

Steps	What It Might Sound/Look Like
1 Say what you will model and why.	"Our rules say that we will take care of the supplies in our classroom. I want to show you how to follow that rule when we use glue sticks so that they'll last and we'll always have them available for all the fun projects we'll be doing. Watch and see what you notice."
2 Model the behavior.	Take the top off the glue stick, and slowly and deliberately roll the glue up just enough to use. Then, gently rub a small dab on one scrap of paper and paste it onto another. Keep silent as you do this. Finally, roll the glue back down, replace the top, and store it in the bin.
3 Ask students what they noticed.	"What did you notice about how I used the glue stick?" If necessary, follow up with questions such as "How far did I roll it up? How did I put it on the paper? How much did I use? What did I do when I was finished?"
4 Invite one or more students to model.	"Who can show us how to use the glue stick the same way I did?"
5 Again, ask students what they noticed.	"What did you notice about the way Taj used the glue stick?"
6 Have all students practice.	"During center time today, we're all going to practice taking good care of the glue sticks. I'll be watching and seeing you do all the things we just noticed."
7 Provide feedback.	"At centers, I saw everyone roll the glue stick up a little but not too far. You used just the right amount. You rolled them all the way down before putting the tops on. It looks like we know how to care for these glue sticks!"

INTERACTIVE MODELING FOR GRADES **K–2**

20–25 minutes

How to Tap Rhythm Sticks on the Floor

Steps	What It Might Sound/Look Like
1 Say what you will model and why.	"Today, we're going to use an exciting new instrument, rhythm sticks. I want to make sure that you know how to use them in a way that follows our music room rules—that we will cherish our instruments and each other. I'm going to keep the beat to the song 'Bingo' that we learned last time. Watch to see how I tap my sticks to the music while keeping myself and everyone else safe."
2 Model the behavior.	Sing the song and tap the sticks gently on the floor in rhythm as you chant the letters *b-i-n-g-o*. Then gently set the sticks down.
3 Ask students what they noticed.	"What did you notice about when I used the rhythm sticks and how I used them?" If necessary, follow up with questions such as "What parts of the song did I tap on? Where did I tap the sticks? How did I tap them? What did I do when the song was over?"
4 Invite one or more students to model.	"Who can show us how to use the rhythm sticks the same way I did?"
5 Again, ask students what they noticed.	"What did you notice about when and how Owen played the rhythm sticks?" Repeat Steps 4 and 5 if needed to reinforce learning.
6 Have all students practice.	"Now we're all going to try to play our rhythm sticks while we chant *b-i-n-g-o* and do so safely and in time with the music."
7 Provide feedback.	"That sounded beautiful. You all tapped once for each letter and touched only the floor with your sticks. You were safe and gentle, and you had fun. I think we're ready to try the sticks with a new song!"

INTERACTIVE MODELING FOR GRADES K–2

30–40 minutes

How to Sort Objects and Record the Sorting

Step	What It Might Sound/Look Like
1 Say what you will model and why.	"Today, you're each going to receive a set of objects. Scientists and mathematicians often study objects by putting them into groups or categories. I'm going to take my set of objects and see if I can figure out some ways to group them. Watch and see what I do."
2 Model the behavior. & **3** Ask students what they noticed.	Use a small bag of attribute blocks and sort them into "round" or "have sides" groups. Then, ask students what they noticed. If necessary, ask: "How did I decide what to put in each group?" After students have identified why you sorted the way you did, write in the first box of your recording sheet and say as you write: "round/have sides." Next, ask students what they noticed about how you recorded your results. If necessary, ask about which box you used, how you wrote, and where you wrote within the box. Then sort the blocks according to color and ask students what they noticed about how you sorted. If need be, ask, "How did I decide what to put in each group?" Record results ("red/blue/yellow") in the second box. Again, ask students what they noticed about how you recorded.
4 Invite one or more students to model.	"Who can show us how to sort a group of objects according to their attributes or characteristics the same way I did and then record the results?" Have one student demonstrate one way to sort and record. Then ask a second student to use the same materials and demonstrate and record a different way.
5 Again, ask students what they noticed.	"What did you notice about how Derrick and Tricia sorted and recorded?"
6 Have all students practice.	"Now I'm going to give each of you a bag of blocks and a recording sheet. See how many ways you can sort and how accurately you can record your ideas. I'll check in with you to see how you're doing."
7 Provide feedback.	As you walk among students, point out thoughtful sorting: "I see that you are really thinking about what characteristics these shapes have in common. I think that you are sorting according to size. Am I correct? How are you going to record that on your sheet?" Because young children often struggle with neat recording of results, point out when they have been careful in their recording: "I see that you have neatly written 'three sides' on the left-hand side of your box, 'four sides' in the middle, and 'five sides' on the right. Writing them separately and neatly helps you and others easily see how you sorted."

10 minutes

Using the Bathroom

Steps	What It Might Sound/Look Like
1 Say what you will model and why.	"I want everyone in this class to feel safe and comfortable in the bathroom and to be able to go without taking too much time away from learning. I've already explained the system. Now I'm going to demonstrate it, pretending this sink is the bathroom sink. Watch and see what you notice about how I take care of myself, other people, and the bathroom."
2 Model the behavior.	Pretend to be working at a desk. Then walk quietly to the class cards, remove a card, and place it in the appropriate slot to show that you're leaving the classroom to go to the bathroom. Walk straight to the "bathroom sink" and pretend to wash your hands. Then pretend to use a paper towel to wipe around the sink. Throw the used paper towel into the trash can. Immediately walk back to the cards, put the card back in its "I'm in the classroom" slot, return to desk, and focus on a task.
3 Ask students what they noticed.	"What did you notice about how I took care of myself and the bathroom?" If necessary, follow up with questions such as "How long did the whole thing take? What did I do to make sure the bathroom was in good shape for others? Why does this matter? What did I do when I got back to the room? What was my voice doing?"
4 Invite one or more students to model.	"Who can show us how to walk to the bathroom and use the sink?"
5 Again, ask students what they noticed.	"What did you notice about the way Deon took care of himself and the bathroom?"
6 Have all students practice.	"Today, we'll all have a chance to use the bathroom as we need to. I'll watch and see you use our system. I'll also check on the bathroom every so often to make sure we are wiping off sinks and putting trash in the containers."
7 Provide feedback.	To reinforce students privately: "I saw that you were only gone about three minutes and got right back to work. That's how it's supposed to work!" To reinforce the whole class: "I did a quick check of both bathrooms. It looks as if all of you are keeping them clean. The sink areas are dry and trash is in the trash cans."

Note: If you teach younger grades, you might choose to break down this routine into bite-sized pieces, model each smaller step separately (for example, how to use the card system, how to wash hands, and so on), and do the modeling in the bathrooms with small groups.

INTERACTIVE MODELING FOR GRADES **3–4**

10 minutes

Circling Up at Recess

Steps	What It Might Sound/Look Like
1 Say what you will model and why.	"To make sure everyone is included and understands how to play certain games, we're going to need a system to gather together quickly in a circle on the playground. Mr. Douglas, Mrs. McKay, Ms. Ricardo, and I are going to show you what that looks like."
2 Model the behavior.	Ask a student to act as the teacher and call out, "Circle up." On that signal, quickly form a circle with the "teacher." Be especially careful to model looking out for each other and staying in your own spaces as you get to the circle quickly. Leave about two arm lengths between each person. When the circle is formed, turn and look with anticipation at the "teacher."
3 Ask students what they noticed.	"What did you notice about how we took care of each other as we circled up?" If necessary, follow up with questions such as "How long did it take us? Why does that matter? What did we do once we got there? How much space was there between us?"
4 Invite one or more students to model.	"Who can show us how to circle up in the same way we did?"
5 Again, ask students what they noticed.	"How did these four students take care of each other as they circled up?"
6 Have all students practice.	"Now we're all going to practice circling up. Carefully play tag in this area until you hear the signal. Then show us how to circle up the same way we just demonstrated."
7 Provide feedback.	"You all came really quickly. That's important so that we'll have as much time as possible to play. You also left a good amount of space between you, but not too much, so that our circle was a good size and actually looked like a circle. We're going to play a game now, and then we'll have a chance to practice circling up again."

Note: Even if you don't have recess duty yourself, finding time at the start of the year to work with your students (and with other teachers if possible) on recess skills can help make recess and the rest of the school day more fun and productive for everyone.

30–40 minutes

How to Measure With a Ruler

Note: Before doing this lesson, the teacher read *How Big Is a Foot?* by Rolf Myller aloud to the class to help them understand the importance of accurate measuring and to serve as motivation for their learning.

Steps	What It Might Sound/Look Like
1 Say what you will model and why.	"As the king learned, when we measure, it's important that we do it accurately and precisely. I'm going to show you how to do that by measuring the length of this book. Watch and see what you notice."
2 Model the behavior.	Without talking, carefully line up the ruler with the zero mark at one end of the book. Make sure the ruler is straight across the book and carefully mark the ending spot. Announce the measurement to the class: "Fifteen and a half centimeters."
3 Ask students what they noticed.	"What did you notice about how I tried to be accurate as I measured?" Make sure that students point out how to hold the ruler straight, carefully place it, and figure out the measurement. If students fail to point out that the zero mark was at the edge of the book, ask: "What did you notice me doing on this end to make sure my measurement was correct?"
4 Invite one or more students to model.	"Who can show us how to measure another book the same way I did?"
5 Again, ask students what they noticed.	"What did you notice Kira doing to make sure her measurement was accurate?"
6 Have all students practice.	"Now, we're all going to practice measuring a list of objects in the room. I'll be watching to see how precisely and accurately you use the ruler."
7 Provide feedback.	To reinforce individuals privately: "I noticed you lining up the ruler on the zero and being very exact at the end. That's what it takes for careful, accurate measuring."

INTERACTIVE MODELING FOR GRADES **3–4**

10 minutes

Cleaning Up a Set of Cards

Steps	What It Might Sound/Look Like
1 Say what you will model and why.	"Our rules say that we will respect our learning tools. When we play games with cards, it's important that we put all of them back in a set that's neatly organized. That way, the people using the set next will have what they need. Watch to see how I clean up the cards so they're ready when we need them."
2 Model the behavior.	Spread out the cards as if you had been playing concentration (with some turned up and some turned down). Ask a student to play the teacher role, ring the chime, and give directions to clean up. Then start putting cards in a stack, being careful to turn them so that they all face the same direction. Use a "think-aloud" to say, "I know that we had 30 cards at the start. I'd better count to make sure I still have 30." Count. Then carefully stretch a rubber band around the stack of cards. Finally, gently add your card set to the basket of cards on the math shelf.
3 Ask students what they noticed.	"What did you notice about how I made sure the cards would be ready the next time we need them?" If necessary, follow up with questions such as "How did I stack the cards? Why should they all face the same direction? How did I place the rubber band so that classmates were safe and the cards were in good shape? What did you notice about the way I placed the set of cards in the basket?"
4 Invite one or more students to model.	"Who can show us how to clean up the cards the same way I did?"
5 Again, ask students what they noticed.	"What did you notice about the way Sanae cleaned up the cards?"
6 Have all students practice.	"At math time today, we're all going to play the concentration game we learned. At the end, I'll watch you all clean up the card sets the same way Sanae and I just showed."
7 Provide feedback.	"You all did it! I saw everyone putting the cards in one direction and in a neat stack. I saw pairs working together to count them. And everyone carefully put the rubber band around their set and placed it gently in the basket."

How to Find a Word in the Dictionary

30–40 minutes

Steps	What It Might Sound/Look Like
1 Say what you will model and why.	"Today, we're going to learn how to find a word in a dictionary quickly, so we can figure out how to say it and what it means. I'm going to show you how to do that by looking up the word *nefarious* from our read-aloud yesterday. Watch and see what you notice."
2 Model the behavior.	Display the word *nefarious*. Flip through the dictionary until you get to the *N*'s. Display the page you land on and say: "I know I'm in the right neighborhood because I'm in the *N* section."
	Then move your finger to the guide words on the left-hand page (*none/nonresistance*) and on the right-hand page (*nonresistant/nor*). "Hmm, looks like I need to go backwards." Display a new page with the guide words *nerve/neurasthenia* and *neuraxon/new*. "I know I'm getting close because these guide words all have *ne* at the beginning, like *nefarious*. But, the first word is *nerve*, which comes after *nefarious* because *r* comes after *f*. I'd better go back some more."
	Go backwards until you find the page that has *neck/negation*. "Aha! I know *nefarious* is on this page because the guide words start with *nec* and end with *neg*. *F* falls between *c* and *g*. Let me look—yes, here it is, *nefarious*."
3 Ask students what they noticed.	"What did you notice about how I found *nefarious*?"
	If necessary, follow up with questions such as "What did I do first? How did I know if I needed to go back a page? How did the guide words at the top of the page help me?"
4 Invite one or more students to model.	"Who can show us how to find a word using the technique I showed? The word to find is *bellicose*, which is in the poem we've been reading."
5 Again, ask students what they noticed.	"What did you notice about what Igwe did to find *bellicose*?"
6 Have all students practice.	"Now we're all going to do some practice. I'm going to give you and your partner a copy of 'Ogre Argument' by Douglas Florian. Together, highlight five words from this poem and find them in the dictionary. Write down the words and the page where you find them."
7 Provide feedback.	To reinforce individual students privately: "I see you looking at the first and second letters of the guide words to help you. You are really getting the hang of it." To close the lesson: Ask students what went well during their search and what was tricky. Reflect on these questions as a group.

Note: In a later lesson, this teacher will use Interactive Modeling to teach how to use the entry for the word to figure out its meaning and how to use the word in speaking and writing.

INTERACTIVE MODELING FOR GRADES 3–4

Entering the Art Room Ready to Learn

10–15 minutes

Note: This lesson is a collaboration between an art teacher and a third grade classroom teacher.

Steps	What It Might Sound/Look Like
1 Say what you will model and why.	"Art is an important part of your education, but you have it for only one hour each week. To make sure that our time together is devoted to art, you need to enter the art room quickly and safely. Ms. Chavez and I are going to show you what that looks and sounds like. Watch and see what we do."
2 Model the behavior.	Once the children are seated, both teachers leave the art room and then re-enter. They walk directly to the rug, sit down, and start reading a message and looking at a painting that the art teacher had set up earlier. After a minute or so, they quietly chat about the colors in the painting (the task in the message).
3 Ask students what they noticed.	"What did you notice about how we entered the art room?" If necessary, follow up with questions such as "How did we go to the rug? Did we stop and look at anything on the way? What did we do once we got to the rug? How did we talk so that we took care of ourselves and others?"
4 Invite one or more students to model.	"We need two volunteers to show us how to enter the art room and go to the rug the same way we did."
5 Again, ask students what they noticed.	"What did you notice that Isabel and Xavier did?"
6 Have all students practice.	"Now we're all going to practice. Pretend it's the beginning of art class. Go back into the hall, and then enter the room and go to the rug the same way we showed you."
7 Provide feedback.	"You all came in quickly and safely. Everyone walked straight to the rug and sat down. You read the message and looked at the painting. You talked quietly with those around you. It looks like we'll have lots of time for art this year. Now, let's talk as a group about what you noticed about the painting."

INTERACTIVE MODELING FOR GRADES 3–4

20–30 minutes

How to Throw a Ball Overhand

Steps	What It Might Sound/Look Like
1 Say what you will model and why.	"In our new PE unit, we're going learn a proper technique for throwing overhand. I want to make sure that you know how to throw the ball so that you can take care of your body and accurately throw the ball to the person who's catching it. Watch to see what I do as I throw this ball."
2 Model the behavior.	Using a Koosh ball, demonstrate proper form in throwing (arm back, elbow bent, step forward with opposite foot from throwing arm, extend elbow as you bring arm past head, and release ball as you step forward with the same foot).
3 Ask students what they noticed.	"What did you notice about what I did with my arms, legs, and hands as I threw the ball?" If necessary, follow up with questions such as "Where did my arm start? What was my elbow doing? When did I let the ball go? What were my feet doing?" Repeat the demonstration if students missed a key aspect of the throwing motion.
4 Invite one or more students to model.	"Who can show us how to throw the ball the same way I did?" (Call on a student or two with whom you practiced beforehand.)
5 Again, ask students what they noticed.	"What did you notice about the way Jazmin threw the ball?" If needed, have a second student demonstrate and ask what classmates noticed.
6 Have all students practice.	"I'm now going to put you in pairs so that everyone can practice throwing to a partner."
7 Provide feedback.	To reinforce individually (in private): "I see you starting behind your head with your elbow bent. That's exactly how to start." Or "I see you straightening your arm and letting the ball go when it gets past your head." To reinforce the whole class: "Lots of people were trying to do exactly what I showed. I especially noticed you getting your feet, arms, and hands in the proper positions before throwing. We'll keep practicing, but we're off to a great start!"

INTERACTIVE MODELING FOR GRADES 5-6

15-20 minutes

How to Cut and Paste Text on a Computer

Steps	What It Might Sound/Look Like
1 Say what you will model and why.	The technology teacher reminds students that they already know how to cut and paste from stories they've handwritten in class. Then she says, "I'm going to show you how to highlight a section of text and move it somewhere else in your file. Watch what I do. Pay close attention to where I put the cursor and what I do with the mouse."
2 Model the behavior.	Demonstrate all the steps involved in cutting and pasting text in a document as students watch.
3 Ask students what they noticed.	"What did you notice about how I moved the text?" If necessary, follow up with questions such as "How did I do that? What did I do next? What exactly did I do to move the text? What exactly did I do with the left-click?"
4 Invite one or more students to model.	"Who can show us how to cut and paste a sentence the same way I did?"
5 Again, ask students what they noticed.	"To help us remember exactly how to do this, let's see if we can describe what we saw Kimee do *in order* from beginning to end."
6 Have all students practice.	"I put a poem you have read before on each computer. In pairs, cut and paste the sentences to make a brand new poem. Your challenge is to keep doing this until I say stop. Then we'll read our 'new' poems together. Be sure to take turns moving each sentence."
7 Provide feedback.	To reinforce individual pairs (in private): "Yes! I see you remembering to move the cursor to the beginning of the text." To reinforce the whole class: "It looks as if everyone knows the steps for cutting and pasting. Tomorrow, you'll have a chance to practice on your own."

10 minutes

How to Make a Smooth Transition from Independent Work to the Circle

Steps	What It Might Sound/Look Like
1 Say what you will model and why.	"I want to make sure we have a smooth clean-up time and transition back to the rug. It's important that this process be quick so that most of our time will be devoted to talking about what we learned. Watch how I do this clean-up and transition."
2 Model the behavior.	Sit at a desk (prepared with a textbook, paper, and a pencil). At your direction, have a student ring the chime. Give your attention, and have the student say, "Time to clean up." Quickly put the textbook in the desk and the pencil in the holder, point down. Get up and put the paper in the finished work basket. Walk to the rug and take a seat. Quietly chat with a person next to you. (You may also want to have music playing during the transition.)
3 Ask students what they noticed.	"What did you notice about how I cleaned up and came to the rug safely and quickly?" If necessary, follow up with questions such as "How did I put the textbook in the desk? How did I put the pencil in the pencil holder? Where did I put my paper? What path did I take to get back to the rug? Why is it important to come directly to the rug? What did I do when I got there? About how long did this whole process take?"
4 Invite one or more students to model.	"Who can show us how to clean up and move to the rug as safely, carefully, and quickly as I did?"
5 Again, ask students what they noticed.	"What did you notice about how Alina cleaned up and went to the rug?"
6 Have all students practice.	"Now I'm going to give you all a ten-minute scavenger hunt to use to explore your social studies textbook. When time is up, I'm going to ring the chime and watch all of you clean up and go to the rug the same way Alina and I did."
7 Provide feedback.	"I saw people putting textbooks carefully into desks, pencils in cups with points down, and scavenger hunts into the finished work basket. I also noticed that you came to the rug directly and fairly quietly. The whole process took you only two minutes, the length of the song. That's going to leave us plenty of time to reflect on and share what we learned."

INTERACTIVE MODELING FOR GRADES 5–6

5–10 minutes

How to Safely Refill a Stapler
(after having modeled how to use the stapler)

Steps	What It Might Sound/Look Like
1 **Say what you will model and why.**	"Our rules say that we will be safe and treat our materials well. I want to show you how to be safe and take care of the stapler when it is out of staples. This way, you'll be able to use it whenever you need it. See what you notice about how I safely add staples to the stapler."
2 **Model the behavior.**	Empty the stapler before the lesson. To start the demonstration, hold the base of the stapler and open up the top slowly and carefully. Silently show students that the stapler is empty. Then carefully take a block of staples, hold back the spring, and add the staples with prongs down. Carefully move fingers out of the way and close the stapler.
3 **Ask students what they noticed.**	"What did you notice about how the staples go into the stapler? How did I take care of my hands and fingers as I put the staples in?" If necessary, follow up with questions such as "What did you notice about what I did when I opened the stapler? What did you notice about what I did to make sure the staples fit? Where was my hand when I closed the stapler?"
4 **Invite one or more students to model.**	"Who can show us how to add staples in the same safe and careful way I did?"
5 **Again, ask students what they noticed.**	"What did you notice about the way Jamar added staples?"
6 **Have all students practice.**	"During writing time today, I'm going to call small groups over to practice adding staples to the stapler."
7 **Provide feedback.**	To reinforce each small group: "I saw everyone opening the stapler carefully, pulling the spring back so that your fingers were safe, and putting the staples in with prongs down. It looks like we're ready to add this tool to our writing center."

INTERACTIVE MODELING FOR GRADES 5–6

10–15 minutes

How to Disagree Respectfully During a "Turn and Talk" (partner chat)

Steps	What It Might Sound/Look Like
1 Say what you will model and why.	"We all learn better when we share our ideas with other people and hear their ideas as well. Sometimes you may disagree with your partner. When you disagree, you need to take care of yourself and your partner. John and I are going to show you what that looks like by talking about whether *Toy Story* is a great movie or not. Watch and see what we do."
2 Model the behavior.	Sit face-to-face and knee-to-knee with a partner whom you have prepared beforehand. Let your partner start by saying why *Toy Story* is a great movie. For example: "People of all ages enjoy it, and it has a great message of friendship. It's funny and easy to watch again and again."
	Show attentive listening as the student speaks and then show some disagreement: "I hear what you're saying, and I do know many people like seeing it again and again, but I disagree that it's a great movie. To me, a great movie is one that's complicated and makes me keep thinking long after it's over. I enjoy watching *Toy Story*, but I rarely think about it afterward."
3 Ask students what they noticed.	"What did you notice about our conversation?"
	If necessary, follow up with questions such as "How did John and I take care of each other during our talk? How did we show we were listening? How did I state my disagreement? What did John do as I disagreed? What was our tone of voice? Why does this matter?"
4 Invite one or more students to model.	"Let's see if we can have two volunteers partner chat about whether a different movie is great. Let's try *Harry Potter and the Sorcerer's Stone*. One of you say, 'Yes, it's great,' and the other disagree."
5 Again, ask students what they noticed.	"What did you notice about Chandra and Simi's partner chat? How did they take care of each other even though they disagreed?"
6 Have all students practice.	"Now we're all going to have a chance to practice. I have listed your partners on this chart. You're going to turn and talk about one of these movies. Choose just one. If possible, try to disagree."
7 Provide feedback.	Signal for quiet attention and then ask, "What did you notice your partner did well, especially in terms of disagreeing?"
	After children reflect, point out any positives you noticed: "You were looking at and listening to your partners. I heard people make their movie sound interesting without giving too much information. People were expressing their opinions using calm voices and respectful words."

INTERACTIVE MODELING FOR GRADES 5–6

10 minutes

How to Store a Tablet Computer on a Cart

Steps	What It Might Sound/Look Like
1 **Say what you will model and why.**	"Our rules say that we will take care of our learning tools. One important tool is the set of tablets we have just used. We have to make sure we return them to the mobile cart carefully and store them properly so that they will be charged and ready for the next class. Watch and see how I place my tablet on the cart."
2 **Model the behavior.**	Model shutting down the tablet. Then carefully carry it over to the cart. Check for your correct number slot and slide the tablet in vertically, facing in the right direction. Then return to your seat and take out a book to read.
3 **Ask students what they noticed.**	"What did you notice I did to take care of the tablet as I went to the cart and put it in?" If necessary, follow up with questions such as "How did I carry it? How did I make sure I got it in the right spot? What direction is it facing? What did I do when I finished?"
4 **Invite one or more students to model.**	"Who can show us how to shut down their tablet and put it in the cart the same way I did?"
5 **Again, ask students what they noticed.**	"What did you notice about the way Andre took care of his tablet?"
6 **Have all students practice.**	"Now I'm going to call you table by table to put your tablets away. I'll be watching and seeing how you take care of them."
7 **Provide feedback.**	"I saw everyone carrying the tablets with both hands and watching where you were going. You checked to make sure you put your tablet in your numbered slot, and you all made sure it was facing the correct direction. I know Ms. Pitt's class will appreciate how well you took care of the tablets."

How to Give a Partner Feedback

20–25 minutes

Steps	What It Might Sound/Look Like
1 Say what you will model and why.	Begin by exploring this question: "Why will it be important to give each other feedback on our writing this year?" Based on responses, you might say, "So when we give feedback, it's important to be honest and take care of each other at the same time. We're going to use a piece of writing from last year. I'm going to pretend I'm giving feedback. Watch and see what you notice I do."
2 Model the behavior.	Have everyone read a couple of paragraphs from the writing sample (delete any identifying characteristics in advance). Then say (pretending to speak to the writer), "You have a great beginning. That sentence, 'Why can't people mind their own business?' made me want to keep reading. I also thought it was really funny how your grandmother always told you that if you didn't have something nice to say, you shouldn't say anything, but that she never followed that advice herself. It made me think of my grandfather. I'm wondering why your friend said you should choose a sport other than baseball to play. I hope you're going to explain that part."
3 Ask students what they noticed.	"What did you notice about the way I gave feedback?" If necessary, follow up with questions such as "How did I take care of my partner while I gave feedback? How would you describe the balance I struck between giving positive feedback and a suggestion for improvement? What was my tone like? Why might that matter?"
4 Invite one or more students to model.	"To sum up, when we give feedback, we want to focus on the positives. If we do have a suggestion, we want to say it carefully, so the person can still feel positive about his or her writing. Who wants to try doing those things with another piece of writing from last year?"
5 Again, ask students what they noticed.	"What did you notice that Candace did to focus on the positives and make her suggestion in a way that felt helpful, not critical?"
6 Have all students practice.	Give each student a sample of an anonymous student's writing. Pair students up and coach them in giving feedback about the sample.
7 Provide feedback.	To reinforce individual pairs: "I noticed that you two are really focusing in on what you like about the writing. That's so helpful because it lets writers know what's working well." To reinforce the whole class: "Everyone worked hard to balance positive feedback with suggestions for improvement. Giving helpful feedback is very hard, even for adults, so we're going to practice one more time tomorrow before we try with each other's writing."

Relevant Research

Interactive Modeling engages students in active learning through modeling, observing, responding, and coaching. Many studies have been done that support such teaching practices.

Here is a small sampling:

Bandura, A. (1977). *Social Learning Theory* (and other works by this author). Englewood Cliffs, NJ: Prentice-Hall. Supports the idea that humans learn by imitating what they see, not by trial and error. When children pay attention to a model, can retain and imitate what they see, and receive positive feedback about their behavior, they are better able to develop that behavior.

Ericsson, K. A., Prietula, M. J., & Cokely, E. T. (2007). The Making of an Expert. *Harvard Business Review, 85*, 114–121. Explains how strong performance in a skill area results from deliberate practice and coaching, not innate talent.

Jensen, E. (2005). *Teaching with the Brain in Mind* (Rev. 2nd ed.). Alexandria, VA: ASCD. Summarizes recent research on the brain and what it means for teachers, including recommendations that teachers actively engage students, provide them with interesting practice or repetition to learn skills, and plan effectively so that students remember the key points of a given lesson.

Marzano, R. J. (2007). *The Art and Science of Teaching*. Alexandria, VA: ASCD. Summarizes research on effective teaching practices, including the power of stopping during demonstrations to ask students for their observations or when practicing a procedural skill. The author also presents research showing the importance of teaching and learning routines and procedures in the classroom.

Paul, A. M. (2012, February 29). Couch Potatoes, Rejoice! Learning Can Be Passive. *Time.* Discusses in lay terms how a circuit in the brain, called the "action observation network," is activated when people watch a process with the intention of copying it. For more on this research, see Frey, S. H., and Gerry, V. E. (2006, December 20). Modulation of Neural Activity During Observational Learning of Actions and Their Sequential Orders. *The Journal of Neuroscience, 26,* 13194–13201.

Rizzolatti, G., Fogassi, L., and Gallese, V. (2006, November). Mirrors in the Mind. *Scientific American, 29* (5): 54–61. Explains how the brain contains a subset of neurons (mirror neurons) that are activated both when people do a specific action and when they watch someone else do that specific action. Rizzolatti and his colleagues discovered these neurons while working with monkeys. They noticed that "when one of us grasped a piece of food, the monkeys' neurons would fire in the same way as when the monkeys themselves grasped the food."

Siegel, D. J., and Bryson, T. P. (2011). *The Whole-Brain Child.* New York: Delacorte Press. Provides practical strategies parents and teachers can use to help children thrive based upon the results of recent brain research.

Sousa, D. A. (2011). *How the Brain Learns* (4th ed.). Thousand Oaks, CA: Corwin Press, Inc. Summarizes research on the brain and what that means for teachers, including recommendations for modeling for students step by step, providing students with time to practice what is modeled, and giving them immediate feedback about how they did during the practice session.

✳

About the *Responsive Classroom*® Approach

Interactive Modeling is a practice within the *Responsive Classroom* approach to teaching. Developed by classroom teachers and backed by independent research, the *Responsive Classroom* approach emphasizes social, emotional, and academic growth in a strong, safe, and joyful school community. The goal is to enable optimal student learning.

To learn more about the *Responsive Classroom* approach, see these resources published by Northeast Foundation for Children and available from www.responsiveclassroom.org ■ 800-360-6332.

Engaging Academics: Offering lessons and assignments that are active and interactive, appropriately challenging, purposeful, and connected to students' interests.

> *The Language of Learning: Teaching Students Core Thinking, Listening, and Speaking Skills* by Margaret Berry Wilson. 2014.
>
> *Learning Through Academic Choice* by Paula Denton, EdD. 2005.
>
> *Guided Discovery in a Responsive Classroom* DVD. 2010.

Classroom Management: Setting up and running a classroom in ways that enable the best possible teaching and learning. The *What Every Teacher Needs to Know* K–5 series includes one book at each grade level.

> *What Every Teacher Needs to Know* K–5 series by Margaret Berry Wilson and Mike Anderson. 2010–2011.
>
> *Teaching Children to Care: Classroom Management for Ethical and Academic Growth K–8,* revised ed., by Ruth Sidney Charney. 2002.

Morning Meeting: Gathering as a whole class each morning to greet one another, share news, and warm up for the day ahead.

The Morning Meeting Book, 3rd ed., by Roxann Kriete and Carol Davis. 2014.

80 Morning Meeting Ideas for Grades K–2 by Susan Lattanzi Roser. 2012.

80 Morning Meeting Ideas for Grades 3–6 by Carol Davis. 2012.

Doing Math in Morning Meeting: 150 Quick Activities That Connect to Your Curriculum by Andy Dousis and Margaret Berry Wilson, with an introduction by Roxann Kriete. 2010.

Doing Science in Morning Meeting: 150 Quick Activities That Connect to Your Curriculum by Lara Webb and Margaret Berry Wilson. 2013.

Morning Meeting Messages K–6: 180 Sample Charts from Three Classrooms by Rosalea S. Fisher, Eric Henry, and Deborah Porter. 2006.

99 Activities and Greetings: Great for Morning Meeting . . . and other meetings, too! by Melissa Correa-Connolly. 2004.

Doing Morning Meeting: The Essential Components DVD and viewing guide. 2004.

Morning Meeting Activities in a Responsive Classroom DVD. 2008.

Sample Morning Meetings in a Responsive Classroom DVD and viewing guide. 2009.

Morning Meeting Professional Development Kit. 2008.

Positive Teacher Language: Using words and tone as a tool to promote children's active learning, sense of community, and self-discipline.

The Power of Our Words: Teacher Language That Helps Children Learn, 2nd ed., by Paula Denton, EdD. 2014.

Teacher Language in a Responsive Classroom DVD. 2009.

Teacher Language Professional Development Kit. 2010.

Teaching Discipline: Using practical strategies, such as rule creation and positive responses to misbehavior, to promote self-discipline in students and build a safe, calm, and respectful school climate.

Rules in School: Teaching Discipline in the Responsive Classroom, 2nd ed., by Kathryn Brady, Mary Beth Forton, and Deborah Porter. 2011.

Responsive School Discipline: Essentials for Elementary School Leaders by Chip Wood and Babs Freeman-Loftis. 2011.

Creating Rules with Students in a Responsive Classroom DVD. 2007.

Teaching Discipline in the Classroom Professional Development Kit. 2011.

First Weeks of School: Taking time in the critical first weeks of school to establish expectations, routines, a sense of community, and a positive classroom tone.

The First Six Weeks of School by Paula Denton and Roxann Kriete. 2000.

The First Day of School DVD. 2007.

Classroom Organization: Setting up the physical room in ways that encourage students' independence, cooperation, and productivity.

Classroom Spaces That Work by Marlynn K. Clayton with Mary Beth Forton. 2001.

Movement, Games, Songs, and Chants: Sprinkling quick, lively activities throughout the school day to keep students energized, engaged, and alert.

Closing Circles: 50 Activities for Ending the Day in a Positive Way by Dana Januszka and Kristen Vincent. 2012.

Energizers! 88 Quick Movement Activities That Refresh and Refocus, K–6, by Susan Lattanzi Roser. 2009.

16 Songs Kids Love to Sing (book and CD) performed by Pat and Tex LaMountain. 1998.

Preventing Bullying at School: Using practical strategies throughout the day to create a safe, kind environment in which bullying is far less likely to take root.

How to Bullyproof Your Classroom by Caltha Crowe. 2012. Includes bullying prevention lesson plans.

Solving Behavior Problems With Children: Engaging children in solving their behavior problems so they feel safe, challenged, and invested in changing.

> *Solving Thorny Behavior Problems: How Teachers and Students Can Work Together* by Caltha Crowe. 2009.

> *Sammy and His Behavior Problems: Stories and Strategies from a Teacher's Year* by Caltha Crowe. 2010. (Also available as an audiobook.)

Working With Families: Hearing parents' insights, helping them understand the school's teaching approaches, and engaging them as partners in their children's education.

> *Parents & Teachers Working Together* by Carol Davis and Alice Yang. 2005.

Child Development: Understanding children's common physical, social-emotional, cognitive, and language characteristics at each age, and adapting teaching to respond to children's developmental needs.

> *Yardsticks: Children in the Classroom Ages 4–14*, 3rd ed., by Chip Wood. 2007.

> *Child Development Pamphlets* (based on *Yardsticks* by Chip Wood; in English or Spanish). 2005 and 2006.

To Learn More:

➻ Visit **www.responsiveclassroom.org** for additional information, including free articles, blogs, and video clips.

➻ Go to **www.responsiveclassroom.org/interactive-modeling** to see video clips of Interactive Modeling in action in real classrooms, or scan the code to go there now.

——— Acknowledgments ———

※

While working on this book, I was fortunate to spend time in many classrooms with teachers and children who helped keep my writing grounded and meaningful. Thanks especially to the staff, teachers, and students of SOAR Charter Schools in Denver, Colorado, New Heights Charter School in Los Angeles, California, and Hillbrook School in Los Gatos, California. Thanks also to all the teachers, administrators, and educators who have inspired me by participating in *Responsive Classroom* workshops over the years—I can't adequately tell you what a powerful impact you've had on my teaching, writing, and understanding of Interactive Modeling.

Kerry O'Grady and Babs Freeman-Loftis, my work buddies and personal cheerleaders, graciously read many drafts and shared ideas throughout the writing of this book. They always inspire me to do my best work, and make learning and working so joyful. Thanks also to Mike Anderson, Carol Davis, Mark Emmons, Sarah Fillion, Lynn Majewski, Rose Monterosso, and Tina Valentine for sharing many ideas and ways that they used Interactive Modeling in their classrooms.

Thanks to Karen Casto, Roxanne Rose, Hannah Whitaker and all the other readers, who provided critical feedback that immeasurably improved the book. Thanks also to Mary Beth Forton, who gave me wisdom, support, and guidance along the way, and to Elizabeth Nash, who read the book with a careful eye and who has always shown me such personal kindness.

My amazing editor, Jim Brissette, kept my writing focused, organized, succinct, and relevant to readers. Alice Yang, as always, gracefully, but honestly, provided editorial wisdom and guidance to both Jim and me. And Helen Merena made the book beautiful and reader-friendly.

Jen Audley, in ways too numerous to list, has made me a better thinker and writer. I tried to channel her often as I wrote this book.

Thanks also to Kathy Woods, whose model I always try to emulate; to Paula Denton, who first taught me about Interactive Modeling and so much more, and is always an inspiration; and to Lara Webb, who continues to encourage me as a writer, teacher, and person.

And personally, I send much thanks and love to Andy, Matthew, and my family. Andy and Matthew make me laugh and help keep things in perspective for every project I take on, and the writing of this book was no exception.

Margaret Berry Wilson has used the *Responsive Classroom*® approach to teaching since 1998. She worked for fifteen years as a classroom teacher in Nashville, Tennessee, and San Bernardino, California, before becoming a *Responsive Classroom* consultant.

Margaret is the author of a number of *Responsive Classroom* books, including *The Language of Learning: Teaching Students Core Thinking, Listening, and Speaking Skills* (2014); *Doing Math in Morning Meeting: 150 Quick Activities That Connect to Your Curriculum* (with co-author Andy Dousis, 2010); and *Doing Science in Morning Meeting: 150 Quick Activities That Connect to Your Curriculum* (with co-author Lara Webb, 2013). She lives in Riverside, California, with her husband, Andy, and their son, Matthew.

--------- About the Publisher ---------

Northeast Foundation for Children, Inc., a not-for-profit educational organization, is the developer of *Responsive Classroom*®, an evidence-based education approach associated with greater teacher effectiveness, higher student achievement, and improved school climate. *Responsive Classroom* practices help teachers develop competencies in four interrelated domains: engaging academics, positive community, effective management, and developmentally appropriate teaching. We offer the following resources for educators:

Professional Development Services

- Workshops for teachers and administrators (locations around the country and on-site)
- On-site consulting services to support implementation
- Resources for site-based study
- National conference for school and district leaders

Publications and Resources

- Books and videos for teachers and school leaders
- Professional development kits for school-based study
- Website with extensive library of free articles: www.responsiveclassroom.org
- Free newsletter for educators
- The *Responsive*® blog, with news, ideas, and advice from and for educators

For details, contact:

Responsive Classroom®

Northeast Foundation for Children, Inc.
85 Avenue A, P.O. Box 718
Turners Falls, Massachusetts 01376-0718

800-360-6332 ■ www.responsiveclassroom.org
info@responsiveclassroom.org